D0611585

LYRICS OF THE
FRENCH RENAISSANCE

Lyrics of the French Renaissance

∞

Marot, Du Bellay, Ronsard

English versions by Norman R. Shapiro
Introduction by Hope Glidden
Notes by Hope Glidden and Norman R. Shapiro

THE UNIVERSITY OF CHICAGO PRESS ∞ CHICAGO AND LONDON

The University of Chicago Press, Chicago 60637
The University of Chicago Press, Ltd., London

© 2002 by Yale University
All rights reserved.

First published by Yale University Press, 2002
University of Chicago Press paperback edition 2006

Publication of this work has been aided by a grant from the
Thomas and Catherine McMahon Fund of Wesleyan University, established
through the generosity of the late Joseph McMahon.

Printed in the United States of America

15 14 13 12 11 10 09 08 07 06   1 2 3 4 5

ISBN-13: 978-0-226-75052-1 (paper)
ISBN-10: 0-226-75052-3 (paper)

Library of Congress Cataloging-in-Publication Data

Lyrics of the French Renaissance : Marot, Du Bellay, Ronsard /
English versions by Norman R. Shapiro ; introduction by Hope
Glidden ; notes by Hope Glidden and Norman R. Shapiro.
    p. cm.
  ISBN-13: 978-0-226-75052-1 (pbk. : alk. paper)
  ISBN-10: 0-226-75052-3 (pbk. : alk. paper)
    1. French poetry—16th century—Translations into English.
I. Shapiro, Norman R.   II. Glidden, Hope H.   III. Marot, Climent,
1495?–1544. Selections. English & French (Middle French).   IV. Du
Bellay, Joachim, 1525 (ca.)–1560. Selections. English & French (Middle
French).   V. Ronsard, Pierre de, 1524–1585. Selections. English &
French (Middle French).
  PQ1170.E6L97   2006
  841'.040803—dc22

                                          2006011872

⊖ The paper used in this publication meets the minimum requirements
of the American National Standard for Information Sciences—Permanence
of Paper for Printed Library Materials, ANSI Z39.48-1992.

To the happy memory of Morton Briggs,
longtime colleague, timeless friend.

CONTENTS

Joachim Du Bellay

Pierre de Ronsard

PREFACE

No excuse should be necessary for translating great poets into English verse. Unless, that is, one needs a rationale for the translation of poetry in general. Some very respectable critics and lay readers see no point at all in the endeavor, feeling that it is really quite impossible, that too much is inevitably lost in the process, and that whatever one comes up with, no matter how skillfully, is only a shadow—or, in more appropriately auditory terms, an echo—of the original. I don't want to rehash a long-standing controversy. Whatever I or others argue, the disciples of Nabokov will continue to assert that only the message can be more or less adequately transmitted, and that even that is possible only by means of a scrupulous, word-for-word rendition replete with glosses and notes explaining the subtleties, nuances, allusions, and so on for the reader unfamiliar with the language of the original, and who wants only to know "what the poem says," not how that content can be artistically reordered—adapted?—into another language.

Myself, I feel that such naysayers would, in fact, be right if only one could accept what seems to be their premise; namely, that a literary translation (of anything, but especially of a poem) must be a precise *duplication* of the work in question. But clearly, that premise is an impossibility. No translation can ever be an exact reproduction, unto every last nuance. What it can and should be, however, is a work in its own right, quite able to stand by itself, but intimately related to the original—it would not exist without it, though it should be able to do so—with its message left intact and as much of its admittedly intangible spirit carried over as well: the two elements that Seamus Heaney, referring to some of my previous translation efforts, has aptly termed "the tune and the tone."

This means, for example, that if rhyme and meter are part of the originals, part of how the poet conceived them, they will be part of my versions as well. If their form is obvious, I will preserve it. (I would find it as jarring to translate a formal sonnet into, say, octosyllabic couplets as to render it in free verse.) If they date from a somewhat remote period, I will avoid jazzing them up with contemporary English or slang, unless I am obviously aiming at "modern dress" or parody. And if they exploit certain specific rhetorical features—repetitions, apostrophes, figures of speech—I will try to maintain those, too. All this, as I say, not in a fruitless effort to *duplicate* the original but to present a poem that clearly acknowledges its debt to it and that, without attempting a slavishly precise rendition doomed from the start to gracelessness, transmits to the sensitive reader an aesthetic mood similar to—again, not *exactly* the same as—the one experienced by a reader of that original.

For some, the preceding remarks will be preaching to the choir. For others, I am afraid they will be the unconvincing attempt of a practitioner of futility to justify the well-meaning but delusionary principles of his craft. So be it.

I undertook the present collection a couple of years ago after publication of another volume. While doing some of the office-cleaning that, for me, inevitably follows such an agreeable gestation, I came across some offprints, not quite yellowing with age but getting there, and recalled that several decades ago the late Professor Milton Goldberg had invited me, then something of a fledgling, to contribute a few translations from the French for a special Renaissance issue of the *Antioch Review*. A handful of versions of Marot, Du Bellay, and Ronsard were the result. A few, in fact, had already served, a year

before, as program translations for a choral concert at Amherst Col-
lege of settings by Harvard composer John Crawford. Rescuing them
from the obscurity of my drawer these many decades later and look-
ing them over, I decided that perhaps more of the same would pro-
vide a worthy effort. They would also pleasantly feed the mild addic-
tion that literary translation—something of a "gentle madness," like
book collecting—has become for me. (When I was a grade-school
pupil, one of my teachers—Esther White? Eloise Fitzgerald?—used
to put inspirational messages on the blackboard for the class to mem-
orize, one of which has stayed with me: "Count that day lost whose
low-descending sun / Views from thy hand no worthy action done."
In recent years I seem to have substituted "no new translation" for
"no worthy action.") Those original translations, somewhat revised,
were, over the succeeding months, joined by the rest of the collection
that I offer to my readers today.

It is with thanks to many that I do so. Always first and foremost, to
my late mother, for instilling in me a love and appreciation of poetry;
to the late Milton Goldberg, for unwittingly setting this project in
motion, albeit long held in suspended animation; to Evelyn Singer
Simha, ever the indispensable listener, whose unfailing aesthetic
judgment, unstintingly offered, has, here as in other works, proven
indispensable and who has more than earned my dedication; to Ben-
jamin Weiss, for much help in seeking out appropriate illustrations,
and to Steve Sylvester and Carver Blanchard for facilitating their use;
to Caldwell Titcomb, always willing to put his encyclopedic knowl-
edge at my disposal; to Seymour O. Simches, a constant source of
inspiration, and to Sylvia and Allan Kliman, a constant source of
encouragement; to Adams House, Harvard University, in the persons
of Robert and Jana Kiely, its former masters, Judith and Sean Palfrey,
their successors, its unequaled dining-hall staff, and Vicki Macy, for
much generous and productive hospitality; to Rita Dempsey and
Carla Chrisfield, for their congenial patience beyond the "calls" of
duty; to Rosalind Eastaway, Susan Ferris, and their several student
assistants, for excellent clerical help; and to Jonathan Brent, Aileen

Novick, Laura Jones Dooley, and Charles Pendergast, of Yale University Press, for their confidence and much hard work in making this collection a reality.

And, of course, my very special appreciation to Hope Glidden for expertly putting her graceful erudition at the service of this volume, with happy result, both in her judicious amplification of my notes and in her superb introduction.

NORMAN R. SHAPIRO

INTRODUCTION

Les Muses viennent à présent pour habiter en France.
                    —Jacques Peletier, *Art poétique* (1555)

Renaissance lyric found its inspiration in multiple sources: Catullus, Ovid, Martial; Anacreon and the *Greek Anthology*; the love sonnets of Petrarch; Neoplatonism; and its own native ballads, rondels, and songs. Clément Marot, Joachim Du Bellay, and Pierre de Ronsard did not model their work slavishly on inherited tradition; rather, they shared the aesthetics of their time, believing that innovation took place only within self-conscious imitation of authors whose works constituted the classical canon. For moderns, it is strange to think that poetry would vaunt its originality through an aesthetic of imitation. How, we may ask, can innovation emerge when poets strive to replicate their predecessors, often borrowing their very words if not producing translations they subsequently passed off as their own? The question of imitation is related to another: How did lyric poets establish a voice, that is, their own authority, in an era that believed that all had already been said, and better, by ancient bards?

The clue to the puzzle is found in the etymology of the word *Renaissance* itself, because it expresses rebirth, or a second coming, of ancient culture. Coined by Jacob Burckhardt in the late nineteenth century, the word *Renaissance* nevertheless captures the youthful drive of poetry in the period 1520–1590, in which springtime and lust combine with irony to sing of love's fortunes. Indeed, a poet such as Agrippa d'Aubigné would write a collection called *Le Printemps* late in the 1560s, the decade when the religious wars turned bloody following the failed truce of 1562.

Throughout the sixteenth century, French writing is conscious of its break with the "age of the Goths," as François Rabelais termed the scholastic past. Beginning with Marot's *Adolescence clémentine,* the French language also emerged from its medieval dialects to begin its evolution into a syntactically coherent language. As late as the 1580s, French writers spelled the same word on one page variously; the normalization of French proceeded slowly, and in the interval, Marot in particular profited from the slippage between oral and written forms to create a lighthearted verse defined by its play with words. Beginning in the 1520s, during the first wave of humanism, Marot practiced the homegrown genres of the ballad, rondel, and song, whose levity made them pleasant to perform and whose natural rhythms he raised to an art. Put another way, he achieved consummate "naturalness" by portraying romance without recourse to Greek and Roman mythology, whose gods later elevated the Pléiade's verse to cosmic dimensions. Like Du Bellay and Ronsard, Marot defended the French language as a vehicle of poetic expression, whereas Latin was still thought by some humanists to be more nuanced and rich in its vocabulary. A vigorous Neo-Latin poetry thrived in sixteenth-century France, but even when Marot adopts the epigram in the manner of Martial, he seems content with the "cruel heart" of fate so long as his "fine damosel" inhabits the city of Paris. With Marot, it may be said that modern French hit its stride by demonstrating how versatile French could be in its variety of genres, from the epistle, epigram, and elegy, to the lyrical rendition of the *Psaumes,* in Marot's translation, by all estimation one of the most exemplary uses of the French language. Apparently without pretension, Marot also served his king as a chronicler, and one may detect in his verse the stirrings of a defense of French that was to become the hallmark of national identity in later years.

French lyric verse owes its motifs to the arrival in France of Pe-
trarch's *Canzoniere,* or *Rime sparse,* the first poetic sequence to be
written entirely in sonnets. Published in Lyon in 1545 by the human-
ist printer Jean de Tournes, the edition contains a dedication to the
Neoplatonist poet Maurice Scève. A second edition by Tournes ap-
peared in 1550, and this one contained a letter from the editor to
Scève on the poet's discovery of Laura's tomb near Avignon in 1533.
By all accounts, this event created the impetus to write sonnets
among people even at the highest level, for King François I also wrote
an epitaph, a commemorative poem, to Laura. Lyon was already
famous in the 1550s for its prosperity, with splendid houses, galleries,
and courtyards showing the penetration into France of Italian archi-
tecture. The city had a large Florentine community, or "nation," of
merchants and financiers, and the architect Philibert Delorme had
built there on his return from Italy. The Italian readership of Lyon was
just one factor that prompted the printing presses to disseminate
Petrarch's poetry. Numerous other editions of Petrarch's *Rime* were
to appear between 1550 and 1564 in Lyon in the shop of Guillaume
Roville, attesting to the sustained popularity of Petrarch's verse in
court and in intellectual circles. A French translation of Petrarch
appeared in 1555 in Avignon, and in 1588 Roville brought out a new
edition in Italian with apparatus: a commentary by the poet Bembo
and a *Dictionnaire de rimes.* Moreover, the *Rime*'s publishing history is
in step with love treatises written by such theoreticians as Leone
Ebreo and Pontus de Tyard, who shaped the interplay of Neoplatonic
motifs cast in poetry inspired by Petrarch. Such material helped the
generation of the 1550s, including Ronsard, to acquire the tools of
the trade, such as the intricacies of form and rhyme in the poet
laureate's own work.

Du Bellay's collection *L'Olive* (1549) was the first *canzoniere* made
up of sonnets in French, and his debt to Petrarchan conceits is seen in
L'Olive's passion for the icy fire of the love experience. It was antith-
esis that governed the rhetoric of desire, turning the lover at odds
with himself in a ritualized agony of love's extremes. Already in this
first collection, Du Bellay's penchant for repetition may be tasted in a

series of laments addressed to his weakened faculties: "O faible esprit . . . O cœur ardent . . . ô peines trop certaines" (*L'Olive*, LX). The poet's chill is then teased back into flame, as the poet works upon the *variatio* on the Tuscan's metaphors of fire and ice. Marot, Du Bellay, and Ronsard each passed through what might appear in hindsight the obligatory Petrarchan love clichés. The Du Bellay of *L'Olive* would later write that he had lost the art of petrarchizing ("Contre les Pétrarchistes"), while Ronsard, poet of *Les Amours,* also pretended that the erotics of a Petrarch were too conventional to express his own pain: "Je ne sçauroy, vue ma peine si forte, / Tant lamenter, ne tant pétrarchiser" (*Amours de Cassandre*). The challenge was to resist absorption into a stylized corpus, and that challenge would create in the Pléiade the search for a new voice whose articulation was found in classical poetry and myth. The dialogue with Antiquity removed the temptation to ventriloquize the *Rime,* but it obliged the poet to find his own voice within and beside Antiquity's defining texts. In 1547 Du Bellay had entered the renowned Collège de Coqueret, where he and his friend Ronsard would read Greek and share the same master, the Hellenist Jean Dorat. The erudition acquired at Coqueret, in the Latin Quarter next to the Sorbonne, would prepare Du Bellay to study the monuments of a past glory that still lived whole in the minds of humanists. The dream of recovery turned short, however, and in its place the poet found a culture broken by history and time's ravages. Du Bellay did not "find Rome in Rome," as one of his *Regrets* puts it. Instead, he suffers the shock of dislocation, yearning for home and struggling, like an ancient mariner "at the rudder of a leaking craft" (*Les Regrets,* XXXIV). Before exploring his poetry of exile, it is well to return momentarily to the business of culture, where another ancient city, Lugdunum (Lyon), built the Renaissance on a firm, Roman tradition.

Lyon became the center of poetic production in the 1540s and 1550s, boasting such pre-Pléiade poets as Maurice Scève, Louise Labé, and Pernette Du Guillet. Benefiting from the city's proximity to Italy, and from the collective presence of artists, courtiers, poets, and bankers drawn to Lyon by Catherine de Médicis, wife of King

Henri II (1547–1559), Neoplatonic verse became popular with a wide spectrum of humanists and the emerging middle class, whose interests included the notion that poetry could elevate the soul to harmony with the Good. The celebrated *gradus amoris* (steps to divine love) was articulated in Plato's *Symposium* and later disseminated by Marsilio Ficino in Latin translation and with commentary in late fifteenth-century Florence. One figure of Neoplatonic love, the lovers' exchange of souls in the kiss, would find imitators in Neo-Latin erotic poetry as well as in Marot, Du Bellay, and Ronsard, who took liberties with the cult of love, sometimes submitting it to parody.

Poetry under François I (1515–1547) is inseparable from royal patronage, as indeed it would continue to be under the later monarchs, Henri II, Charles IX, and Henri III, who accorded privileges to their poets in return for flattery. The same was true for the "grand and glorious," or nobles, such as the duc de Guise, to whom Marot addresses a poem in his persona as "Clément, your lowly servant" (*Epistres,* XXIII). The frail valet pleases his master with clever verse so that he may live to write another day. It is known that when Marot was ten years of age, he first entered the court of France, where he followed his father, the poet Jean Marot, into the service of Anne de Bretagne (1505). As a youth, Clément became a servant of Marguerite d'Angoulême, the future queen of Navarre and sister of François I. His career oscillated between light verse and the engaged politics of evangelical writing, the latter bringing charges of heresy that forced him into exile in 1536. Still, Marot benefited from the protection of Marguerite de Navarre and Renée de Ferrare, and it was with their support that he wrote some of his most engaging epistles satirizing the doctrinaire Sorbonne in its fulminations against the evangelical reform movement. The system of patronage under the French monarchy is too complex to analyze here; rather, its power to shape rhetoric deftly is to be noted, so that power may be obtained even as the poet affects to have none. With lady, lord, or creditor, the servant is the master because his words trump the powers that be by making his public smile. Marot's "wizened frame" pleads and ultimately outwits attempts to brand him a Lutheran heretic, even when his accuser is named the Sorbonne and condemns him to the Châtelet prison where he landed in 1526, so the story goes, betrayed by a lady friend for breaking the Lenten fast. This and other anecdotes contribute to the portrait of a Villonesque rogue living on his patrons' handouts, but this, too, is a persona that Marot cultivated through the gaiety of his words.

French Renaissance verse arguably began with Marot, who continued the formal rhyming of the Grands Rhétoriqueurs school, and it is to him as well that the notion of genre may be attributed. A connoisseur of Italian, he had already composed his "Chant des visions de Petrarque, translaté de Italien en François" in 1534, along with select sonnets by Petrarch. In fact, the valet of Marguerite de Navarre had translated not only Petrarch but a range of texts that were indispensable to humanism's program to revive ancient writings. Among these may be counted *Le Premier Livre de la Metamorphose d'Ovide* (1534), four *Eglogues* of Virgil (1536), and the *Trois premiers livres de la Metamorphose* (1556), not to mention his modernized version of the great *Roman de la Rose* (1526). His masterwork of translation is certainly the *Psaumes,* wherein the "naturalness" of his style burgeoned into the lyric simplicity known to be that of King David's original. The growth of French lyric owed much to translation, for it was, in the theorist Jacques Peletier's words, the "cause que la France a commencé à goûter les bonnes choses" (the reason that France started to taste good things; *Art poétique,* 1555). Among those good things, readers found more than a trace of Petrarchan conceits; but also, and majestically, in the 1540s, they discovered Marot's translations of the *Psaumes,* whose songs rang out to the evangelical Christian audience and whose lyricism created a Protestant poetics that rivaled the classicizing odes of a decade later.

The normative reading of Renaissance lyric impresses the reader with lyric's formal motifs, even clichés, that repeat endlessly the awakening of love as a wound that paralyzes the lover-victim, rendering him mute. On one level this impression is not wrong, but the amorous code also sets up the conditions for combustion to occur, itself a product of passion submitted to time, measure, and the exigency of textual space. French lyric would develop as a *variatio* on the Tuscan poet's fourteenth-century verse; however, a Du Bellay would write of the "sweet prison" (*L'Olive,* XXXIII) of the captive poet and of his lady, his "doulce moitié" (sweet other half). In that Platonic echo lies the novelty of a humanism whose love cannot be imagined outside the Eros of ancient Greece and Rome. Platonic love and the rakish verse of a Catullus speak the Gallic tongue of the 1550s, each inserting its idiom into the Pléiade's new vocabulary.

"Let me count the ways," wrote a sonneteer whose verse worried the how and the why of loving. "How many kisses can be planted on the body of the text?" asked another poet, Jean Second (Johannes Secundus), the Neo-Latin poet whose *Basia* (*Kisses*) shaped the erotic vocabulary of Marot's generation, with its evocation of mouths, tongues, and touching, all groping in a mêlée as methodical as it was violent. In contrast, Marot's "doulx baiser" (sweet kiss) recalls that joy is always fleeting but in tune with the light step of language rejoicing at the grace of lovers' hearts, so gay. This Marot had not yet traversed the crucible of a Catholic Church hungry to eviscerate the evangelical reform movement. Marot was imprisoned in the Châtelet in 1526 and released the year after, but not before he had translated the great erotic masterpiece of the High Middle Ages, the *Roman de la Rose.* This gift to moderns celebrated the "naturalness" of desire, the effect of which was to paganize courtly love into a copulative act. Marot achieved his "naturalness" with consummate mastery of his art. The poet of love lives his fate with seeming *insouciance,* that particularly French practice of flirtation mixed with dread before Fortune's blows.

Marot's Italian contemporary Baldassare Castiglione would set wit (*sprezzatura*) above doctrine as the sign of words' power over chance. In his influential *Book of the Courtier* (Venice, 1528), Castiglione promoted dialogue as the form best suited to philosophy's role in shaping courtly culture. The wit, wile, and ruse of conversation animates the Marotic line as well. The poet surrounds himself gladly with images of lady, mistress, and nymphs, all of which fleet through his poems as yet ungrounded by Antiquity's recycled goddesses. Marot sings the

victim's song when, in Norman R. Shapiro's words, "love pays no
high esteem to loyalty." But the plaint is often tongue-in-cheek, for
Marot would gladly exchange his lady's heart for other pleasures. "Ô
Dieu du Ciel, qu'amour est forte chose" (O God in heaven, how
strong is love), he laments, while knowing too that the lady's cruelty
may end in "ung doulx baiser" (a sweet kiss). Turning not to the
sonnet but to the ballad and late-medieval rondel, he calls on "natu-
ralized" language to eschew the melancholy of elusive love. In an age
when love was fused with melancholy, Marot's desire is nimble; he
chooses not the Petrarchan sonnet but forms whose circular move-
ments and repeated refrains evoke love's recurring pleasures. Far from
creating the "durs épigrammes" that Maurice Scève would write in
the 1540s in Neoplatonic Lyon, Marot writes with a light heart, in
awe that he should so be loved by lady friends.

A revolution in poetry occurred at midcentury, and it is to the
Pléiade, a group of seven lyric poets, that goes the credit for inaugu-
rating a bold new departure in choice of genres and language. Ron-
sard was to publish his Pindaric *Odes* in 1550, and by 1558 Du Bellay
had published four tomes of personal poetry, justifying the percep-
tion that poetry and poetics had changed course. In 1549 Du Bellay
published a treatise, the *Deffense et illustration de la langue françoyse*
(*Defense and Illustration of the French Language*), to demonstrate that
French, albeit a young language, could rival the ancient Latin and
Greek in its poetic excellence. To understand why this theme was so
contested, we may recall a few other points: Du Bellay defended
French against its detractors, those humanists who considered it too
quaint to express deep ideas and feelings; moreover, he stressed that
French would come of age, but only if it emulated classical genres—
hence, the second half of his argument in which "illustrations" of
ancient figures are displayed. In one polemic tract, then, Du Bellay
had discredited the genres based on the medieval past, including, in
his view, Marot's; instead, the vernacular tongue would be trained by
recitation of classical authors, to the end that diction should conform
to the high registers of ancient discourse.

The notion of emulation (*aemulatio*) may be traced, outside classi-
cal theory, to the pedagogical writing of the Dutch humanist Eras-

mus, for whom it kindled the drive for perfection among schoolboys. By challenging each other to strive higher, both subjects would surpass what each could accomplish alone, and the poetic rivalry between Du Bellay and the "others" may arguably be couched in these same terms. Ronsard and Du Bellay both credited poetry as the means to vouchsafe immortality, born of the conviction that writing lasts, even as the body disappears. For both, the laurel crown was superior to worldly goods, and for both, the poet inhabits a superior world whose objects are called, somewhat preciously, the Graces, the muse, the lyre, and whose dramatis personae include satyrs and nymphs. In Du Bellay's world, poets would fly "[d']une esle encor' non usitée" (on a wing as yet untried) (*Vers lyriques,* XIII). Neither historiographic nor merely entertaining, poetry captured the passion for greatness that art could command in a venal world.

Du Bellay was the first poet to introduce the Petrarchan lyric into France as a sonnet sequence in his *L'Olive* (1549). But it was as the polemicist of the *Deffense et illustration de la langue françoyse* that he made an indelible mark on French letters. Stating that all languages were born equal but that some, such as French, were too young yet to rise to excellence, Du Bellay refused to count French among the lesser languages. French's newness should not be held against it as a flaw; rather, French could achieve the complexity of ancient languages given the time to cultivate ancient genres, such as the ode and the elegy. As a discipline, poetic theory drew upon the habits of thought dominant in the age, among which was the use of analogy. Du Bellay points out that Latin masterpieces could not have been written if Greek had not served them as a model; similarly, French could become lofty only by modeling itself on its illustrious predecessors. It was not that some languages were inherently superior to others, either weak or strong by nature; rather, languages were not born but made, achieving greatness through the will of the mortals who cultivated them. Imitation was the strategy to arrive at eloquent verse.

This being said, Du Bellay's theory was also fraught with contradictions, notably the conflict between a native tongue and the loan words crucial to enriching it. Critics did not all endorse the role that the ancient languages played in Du Bellay's language theory. For example, Jacques Peletier would complain in the 1550s that the emerging discourse of French was derivative: Why do we talk through others' mouths? he asked. Why do we disguise our thoughts in borrowed clothing? According to Peletier, for French poets to affirm their own poetics they had to establish rules that liberated their verse from ancient models. In practice, that meant allowing the French language to be *naïf,* so that it resounded with the purity of its native form, or "langage naturel" (*Art poétique*). Ironically, Thomas Sebillet's *Art poétique françoys* (1548), published just one year prior to the *Deffense,* had promoted just that, by celebrating the fixed forms of the medieval *ballade, chant royal, chanson,* and *coq-à-l'âne.* It is clear from hindsight that the revolutionary coup of the Pléiade poets needed a symbolic victim, and in their theory Marot would be the casualty of a poetics that would call itself noble. In sum, the quarrel between the camps would affirm the importance that genre had come to assume in the writing of poetry. To be great, it was indispensable to write in the ancient genres, but also to see the limits of the natural as an end in itself. Tellingly, Du Bellay revisited this issue when he later wrote in the *Deffense* that "le naturel n'est suffisant à celuy qui en poesie veut faire œuvre digne d'immortalité" (naturalness is not sufficient alone for him who in poetry wishes to write a work worthy of immortality). Erudition had its place after all, and to acquire it, the poet needed to keep vigils, "sweat and tremble," and deprive himself of food and drink, in contrast to the excesses of poets deemed merely courtly. Fortunately for its readers, such rigor only enhanced the musicality of a lyric that would charm patrons and readers alike.

From these brief comments, it will be seen that the Pléiade poets fetishized the plume, the Muse, and the lyre, setting the stage for cult worship of the Ancients that included, to be sure, hymns to France's gardens, pastures, and rivers, such as the Loire and the Loir, in Anjou and Touraine. The Pléiade group called themselves the Brigade, a self-conscious band whose members worked to elevate poetry to its rightful status as a sacred medium. Ronsard anointed himself the French Pindar, and it was he who invented in French the Pindaric ode in 1550 to reflect the Greek's variety of meter and rhyme. Ronsard stated in his preface to the *First Book of Odes* (1550) that Pindar's "admirable inconsistencies" guided his own, and this suppleness advanced the French language to a new level of lyric achievement. In the meanwhile, the *Deffense* had established Du Bellay as a brilliant but arrogant critic; in the 1550s he would move inward to the *moi,* whose self was exiled from Anjou to the corrupt world of papal Rome. The Roman collections, *Les Antiquitez de Rome* (1558) and *Les Regrets* (1558), written during Du Bellay's embassy to the Eternal City but published in France upon his return, recount his four years of activity in the entourage of his cousin, Cardinal Jean Du Bellay. The pieces in the dossier are well known: he departs for Rome in 1553, landing first in Rome's Palazzo Farnese, where the cardinal lived, and he lodged there for a time. Du Bellay would leave Rome in August 1557, just as the troops of François de Guise arrived to take the city.

From the vantage point of the disciple of Jean Dorat, the Rome of Catullus, Ovid, and Virgil was an allegory of human grandeur that had decayed into physical (and moral) ruin. The metamorphosis of Rome, her "vices entassez" (heap of vices) (*Les Regrets,* CIX), contrasted perversely with Du Bellay's Anjou, the "douce France," and this praise of his origins conflates the innocence of home—its naturalness—with a nationalism that promotes French identity as a product of its mythic ancestry. In the Eternal City, the poet struggles against the elements "at the rudder of a leaking craft"; the *spiritus* of Rome swells to overpower the solitary voyager, and the mismeasure between the poet and the elements creates the vision, or *energeia,* that overwhelms him. The fictive mariner-poet is drawn into a conflicted state of exaltation and melancholy before the sight of Antiquity's demise, deflated by the sight of temples whose columns have crumbled to the ground. A nineteenth-century traveler to that same city, Stendhal, wrote that experiencing a city is of another order than observing it, because we can never know the world objectively, but only by the effect it has on us: "Je ne prétends pas dire ce que *sont* les choses; je raconte la *sensation* qu'elles me firent" (I do not claim to say what things *are;* I recount the *feelings* they gave me) (*Rome, Naples, Florence,* 1816).

Du Bellay's feelings before the decay of Rome cannot be doubted. He was overwhelmed by the physical ruin of the ancient sites, but just as much by the Vatican and its scandals. Where God resided in the pope, the visitor found the low life of pimps, syphilis, and, of course, the masks of hypocrisy worn by both priests and prelates. What part of Du Bellay's reaction is owed to France's militant defense of the Gallic church, whose autonomy was compromised by papal bulls and taxation alike? The Catholic Council of Trent turned to repression in the 1550s; but Du Bellay's poetry convinces us that, objectively, the hedonism of the Church betrayed its believers, and that issues of politics aside, its vices were such that to mend the Church was to attempt a task equal to cleansing the Augean stables (*Les Regrets,* CIX). The rejection of Rome was coupled, too, with the conviction that ancient models were poetically useless, for poetry was at its most eloquent when it expressed not others' words but the poet's own desire: "Je me contenterai de simplement écrire / Ce que la passion seulement me fait dire" (I will happily limit myself to writing / Only [and simply] what my passion makes me say) (*Les Regrets,* IV). Du Bellay sought communication of an "inner world," so that his subjects impress moderns as particularly "natural" in the way they speak their loss, tinged with the vanity of declaring themselves radically new and, hence, liberated from the overbearing father that was Antiquity.

In this volume, the poems translated from the *Divers Jeux rustiques* portray a Du Bellay who takes flight into an ideal landscape full of the bounty of wheat and grape-rich wine. Written nevertheless during his stay in Rome, they paint the countryside as a vivid tableau of fields and peasants who inhabit them, including Hurauld the sheepdog, raised in Poitou on the banks of the river. The epitaph praises Hurauld because he watched the herds while the other dogs slept, thus becoming a hero in his own right. Such verse reinforces the stated goals of his *Deffense* to "naturalize" poetry and to make it reflect simple feelings. Such poetry would seem to avoid learned allusion, and yet, the *Divers Jeux rustiques* are themselves derivative, in one case, drawing their source from the Neo-Latin poet and diplomat André Navagero (Naugerius), friend of Bembo and Raphael in Rome, and author of the Latin collection *Lusus* (1530), from which poems II– XIII in Du Bellay's collection are taken. Regarded in our century as a plagiarism, Du Bellay's borrowing does not boast originality but rather his gift for absorbing into French the elements it needs to enrich it. The hound Hurauld poem also plays into the thematic of endings, whereby the animal's death signals the continuation of rural violence, in which beasts and robbers will retake possession of "our wealth."

Ronsard's *Second Livre des Amours* also works within a pastoral mode of sorts but uses the country rather as a setting in which to love gently, without social hierarchy. The mistress of his second collec- tion, Marie l'Angevine, transformed the Ovid-like poet from a for- mal sonneteer into a lover of simplicity, as Marie's insouciance valo- rized poetically a shift in register from the high tone of ancient myth to one of shared affection. That was in the mid-1550s. But in 1552 Ronsard listens to the Muses who speak to him not of Cupid but of the "enfant de Cytherée" (child of Cytherea). In that paraphrase lies the mythic world of allusion, replete with pagan mysteries that shaped Renaissance painting, poetry, and the heroic temper that led to describing experience in cosmological terms. Where medieval allegorists had discerned Christian precepts in the amoral cavorting of the gods, humanists enjoyed such works as the *Odyssey* and the *Metamorphoses* without bowing to allegorists' moral glosses. Yet there are no regrets for Ronsard, except perhaps his failure to be the con- quering god that subdues his prey, just as Zeus seized the maidens Danaë, Europa, and Leda of old. His *Amours de Cassandre* (1552) demands to be read as a book of seductions in which the poet fanta- sizes his power to dominate but forgets that the Petrarchan arrows will dart sunbeamlike from the lady's eyes, paralyzing his tongue and reducing him to silence. Thus, the poet creates the fiction of his own impotence, but his failure is matched by the poetic power to evoke passion, in *Cassandre* in Homeric epithets in painterly metaphors, where Cassandra's hair is envisioned as "dawn's ruddy locks in the brightening East." The subsequent collections, *Continuation des Amours* (1555) and *Nouvelle Continuation des Amours* (1556), evoke a flesh that would dissolve, like that of Shakespeare's tormented prince, into the dew of a garden awakening at sunrise. Pierre de Ronsard imagined his beloved Marie as a flowering garden, and if his poems to her did not resonate with allusions to Antiquity's noble maidens, such as Cassandra, they spoke by election to a girl in her province of Anjou.

The choice of beloved probably had less to do with physical attraction than with the poet's desire to experiment with poetic registers. To the mythological verse of *Cassandre,* Ronsard opposed the *beau style bas* (lovely low style) of the *Amours de Marie,* as the continuations were also called, responding to the public's complaint that his poems were obscure, even pedantic. In Marie the poet found relief from poems that were earlier laden with Antiquity's pantheon. Interestingly, the *Amours de Cassandre* had necessitated a gloss to make them intelligible. Marc-Antoine Muret, the humanist and Ronsard's friend, published a commentary on the *Amours de Cassandre,* glossing its learned allusions with the express purpose of making them readable by the non-Latin-reading public. The *Amours* would receive a second commentary in 1560 by the Pléiade poet Rémy Belleau, whose aim was not to popularize but rather to display the erudition that Ronsard had tucked away, thus restoring the poet to his place alongside Anacreon and the poets of the *Greek Anthology.* These editorial efforts would keep Ronsard's *Amours* in play through successive editions, culminating with the first edition of his complete works in 1578.

Like all Renaissance poets, Ronsard bemoaned his passing youth: (my) "douce jouvance est passée" (my sweet youth is fled), he wrote in his *Odes.* But the carpe diem theme was obligatory in a poetics descended from the Roman tradition. In point of fact, Ronsard lived quite well within the career he had chosen: court poet and ecclesiastic. By 1558 he already possessed a priory in Anjou, and during the years 1564–1566 evidence suggests that he had become an affluent

man of letters. Marguerite de France asked her mother, Catherine de
Médicis, to offer him an abbey, and Charles IX, his king and patron,
also gave him an abbey during the 1560s. Comfortably living on his
ecclesiastical income, he continued to produce such important works
as his *Abbregé de l'art poëtique françois* (1565); and not incidentally, it
was on the first of May, 1566, at the court of Charles IX, that he met
his love to be, Hélène de Surgères, the demoiselle in Catherine de
Médicis's court who would be the subject of his final collection of
love poems, the two books of *Sonnets pour Hélène* (1578).

As court poet, Ronsard was also a propagandist for the Catholic
monarchy. In this capacity, he orchestrated public entertainment, and
evidence shows that he collaborated with painters and sculptors, not
to mention set designers, for the most splendid of events, the royal
entry of Charles IX and his queen, Elizabeth of Austria, into Paris in
1571. The peace of Saint-Germain had recently inaugurated a period
of calm in the clashes between Catholics and Protestants; moreover,
Charles's marriage to the granddaughter of the Emperor Charles V,
longtime rival of François I, promised a new age of harmony in the
political sphere.

Ronsard prepared the royal entry and enlisted Jean Dorat to help
him, assuring that its iconography would be a concert of music,
dance, scenery, and pageantry. When the royal couple marched
through the triumphal arches in high ceremony, they stepped to the
beat of a genealogy rooted in Francus, the mythical founder of the
French nation, whose statue stood aloft the arches at the entrance to
the city at Saint-Denis. The monarchy, with the help of Ronsard's
poem, traced its lineage to the son of Hector of Troy, the hero whose
birth was cast as an epic of the French nation. Ronsard's attempt at
epic, his unfinished *La Franciade* (1572), appeared the year after the
royal entry of Charles IX into Paris and includes some of the festive
writing Ronsard had done for the entry. His epic did not achieve the
dignity necessary to rival the gravity of Homer and Virgil, the an-
cient bards. How may we understand this failure, when France
needed a national hymn like the *Iliad,* or so its monarchs thought?
But it is also worth considering whether his age no longer needed to

forge its identity through revival of Homeric heroes. The future of nationhood (and poetry) lay perhaps elsewhere. It is a sad irony that 1572 was also the year of the massacre of Saint Bartholomew's day, in which Protestants were slain, first in Paris near Saint-Germain-l'Auxerrois and later throughout the provinces. The peace staged magnificently in 1571 had now returned to polemics and bloodshed. Hundreds of Protestants had already come to Paris to witness the marriage of Marguerite de France and the future Henri de Navarre celebrated on August 18, 1572, just six days earlier. The tragedy blackened the reputation of Catherine de Médicis, its supposed author, and plunged France further into civil dissolution.

As poet laureate, Ronsard had also written an epitaph upon the death of Anne de Montmorency (1568), celebrated Anjou's triumph over the Protestants at Jarnac (1569), and marked the royal entry of King Henri III into Paris in 1574 following the death of his brother, Charles IX. Ronsard had also been present in 1559 when King Henri II, on his deathbed, ordered the marriage of his daughter Marguerite de France to the duc de Savoie. He obliged the new couple with a "Chant pastoral" (pastoral song). The mystery of the 1570s is that he was able to craft a new sonnet cycle while juggling his church properties, court life, and the obligations that came with serving his king in a ceremonial age. More impressive yet, Ronsard the editor arranged his poems into marketable editions, showing that his business acumen was just as strong as his knack for obtaining commissions. Ronsard oversaw publication of his work in successive editions between 1550 and 1584: he excised poems, reintroduced them, and then rewrote and rearranged them, in effect denying his editions the closure that would have to wait until later editors completed the oeuvre. Modern editions track the stages of the work, publishing the pieces that were edited out ("vers retranchés"), so that the full corpus of the work may remain intact. Shapiro's translations honor this example, including some poems that did not appear in the 1584 edition, the final edition overseen by the poet. Ronsard served his last king, Henri III, until his death in 1585. His *Sonnets à diverses personnes* form a "who's who" of poets, intellectuals, humanists, and courtiers of the end of the Valois reign.

Ronsard is often given credit for creating a public for poetry and, what is more, a poetry that consists of pure feeling. But he was also, like fellow humanists, a theoretician committed to serving Truth, that is, the conviction that imitation as a doctrine was not limited to the rewriting of models but was to include the imitation of Nature herself, the true source of perfection. In his *L'Abbregé de l'art poëtique*, he underscored that the poet's job is to represent, describe, and imitate Nature, and that imitation is the goal of all poetry: "L'invention n'est autre chose que le bon naturel d'une imagination" (Invention is not anything else save the good naturalness of an imagination). The Platonic influence is heard in Ronsard's notion of what the object of imitation is: not the ancients or the Italians, finally, but the "ideas in nature" that lie beyond phenomena in the world. Intellectualized as this dictum might seem, Ronsard's poetry during the years 1574–1585 was increasingly personal, and especially his *Sonnets pour Hélène* confirm that he could still use the alexandrine meter to great emotional advantage. In the *Sonnets pour Hélène,* he experiments again with the canonical vocabulary of Love's arrows, but his language thaws like crystal in a springtime stream, here, the lap of his final love, Hélène, who was by reputation a learned lady of the court. His last sonnet cycle owes its brilliance to an aging body that writes, ruefully, that love is full of "beauteous grace," if not the fire of the Petrarchan martyrdom.

Ronsard's sexual body kept good company with his writing hand throughout his long and prosperous career, producing a work of astonishing breadth and experimentation. Such an oeuvre is stunning to the point that readers may easily decontextualize it, gratified to find therein the universality of feelings they have known and that mortals have experienced in all ages. But if his poems are timeless, the complicity between poet and reader must not be allowed to obscure the landscape of a Renaissance whose ideologies, social world, classifications—in a word, power relations—were vastly different from our own. To take just one example, the Prince of Poets, as the critic Laumonier called Ronsard, saw his work tossed into the bonfire of prohibited books, victim of a censorship that did not see fit to publish "joyeusetez" (entertaining verse) that probably shocked the officially chaste mores of the 1550s. The reference here is to his *Livret de folastries* (1553), a slim volume that contained scatological epigrams and sexual *blasons* (licentious anatomical poems), both of which appear in this volume, whereas the *Folastries* are largely unavailable in anthologies and hence rarely taught. Unwilling to repeat the institutional marginalizing that the priapic poems suffered in the past, the translator offers them here to add texture to the image of a writer whose codified language does not at first glance appear receptive to the countercode of phallic humor.

Ronsard's printer had duly obtained the "privilege to print" the *Folastries,* and yet the books were seized by the authorities bent on preventing their sale. Fortunately for posterity, a few copies escaped the censors, and they find their place today in a work that shared with its age the religious, judicial, and gender politics—to name just a few—that dominated France after the reign of François I, considered retrospectively a golden age of cultural advancement. Were the *Folastries* denounced by Protestant enemies, or did Ronsard break taboos that were beyond the pale for a royal servant of his high position? The editors of the *Pléiade* edition, the most comprehensive French edition of his works, suggest that humanists could write erotic verse with impunity in Latin, whereas the French vernacular was reserved for more comely subjects, thus imposing upon the poet a kind of self-censorship even when official repression did not occur. Ronsard never did avow authorship of the *Folastries.* Be this as it may, the fate of Renaissance writing hinged during the entire sixteenth century, and not only in France, on the vagaries of status and power, as indeed they must in an age of monarchy. A salient testimony to power is found in the request made by Charles IX, the poet's close friend and patron, who asked Ronsard to use the decasyllable meter for his *Franciade* when the dignified alexandrine, the meter of epic, would have been a more appropriate choice.

In the 1530s and 1540s Marot, and later, to a lesser extent, Ronsard, fell victim to religious zealots in the Parliament of Paris and in the Sorbonne, and Du Bellay was in his own way persecuted, too, when his papal colleagues dashed his hope to find in Rome a site of self-renewal. Rather, it was to be in the renewal of poetic *language* that freedom from constraints could be savored, through the imposition of *formal* constraints that elevated speech to become song, all the while creating an effect of naturalness in the most artificial of mediums, lyric poetry. The poems in this collection find voice in an English language that realizes the Renaissance goal of translating— etymologically, "carrying across"—the original in an alchemy of vocabulary and forms. They imitate the source, as they also liberate the imagination. There cannot be a tribute more fitting to the century's conviction that poems, like erudition, are a *translatio studii* (movement of text) from one place to another.

HOPE GLIDDEN

POETA · CLEMENS · MAROTVS · CHAORSIVS

Anté rudis, per te, calamos, infante Thaleia,
Edidicit dulces Gallica lingua modos.

I, 114

Clément Marot

(1496–1544)

Ballades

Rondeaux

Chansons

Elegies

Epistres

Chants divers

Epigrammes

Note: Although different editions present and number
Marot's works in a variety of ways—especially his voluminous
Epigrammes, arranged idiosyncratically by modern editors—I have
followed the ordering and numbering of his works as they appear in the
authoritative edition of Gérard Defaux, *Œuvres poétiques complètes,* 2 vols.
(Paris: Garnier, 1990), cited hereinafter as Defaux. (As for the *Epigrammes,*
it should be noted that their arrangement into four books, not originally
intended by Marot, is largely the editor's doing.) I follow that
edition also in regard to titles, as well as in often divergent
matters of sixteenth-century orthography, capitalization,
punctuation, and line arrangement. [NRS]

BALLADES

D'ung qu'on appeloit frere Lubin

Pour courir en poste à la Ville
Vingt fois, cent fois, ne sçay combien,
Pour faire quelcque chose vile,
Frere Lubin le fera bien.
Mais d'avoir honneste entretien,
Ou mener vie salutaire,
C'est à faire à ung bon Chrestien.
Frere Lubin ne le peult faire.★

Pour mettre (comme ung homme habile)
Le bien d'aultruy avec le sien,
Et vous laissez sans croix, ne pile,
Frere Lubin le fera bien.
On a beau dire, je le tien,
Et le presser de satisfaire,

★The ballade, of which this is an excellent example, obeys a regular disposition of rhyme: three stanzas of eight lines each, followed by an *envoi,* or quatrain. The distinguishing characteristic of the ballade is its refrain, which is repeated after each stanza. The word *ballade* derives from the Old French *baller,* "to dance," and its appearance dates from the thirteenth century. Marot uses the refrain to advantage, underscoring the hypocrisy of the religious orders. [HG]

Of Friar Lubin

To dash to town and have a spree—
A score, a hundred times, or more—
For some foul vice or villainy,
Friar Lubin is there therefor;
But for an honest, godly chore,
A noble act, a just affair,
Righteous and Christian to the core:
Friar Lubin is never there.

To filch another's property
And, shameless, add it to his store,
Down to the last, I guarantee,
Friar Lubin is there therefor;
Ply him with threats, entreat, implore
That he return your rightful share:

Jamais ne vous en rendra rien.
Frere Lubin ne le peult faire.

Pour desbaucher par ung doulx stile
Quelcque fille de bon maintien,
Point ne fault de Vieille subtile,
Frere Lubin le fera bien.
Il presche en Theologien,
Mais pour boire de belle eau claire,
Faictez la boire à vostre Chien,
Frere Lubin ne le peult faire.

Envoy
Pour faire plus tost mal, que bien,
Frere Lubin le fera bien:
Et si c'est quelcque bon affaire,
Frere Lubin ne le peult faire.

Save to deceive you—nay, ignore!—
Friar Lubin is never there.

   To turn a maid of high degree,
With honeyed tongue, to lowly whore,
You need no scheming crone; for he,
Friar Lubin, is there therefor,
Spouting, like churchly orator,
False words, fit for your hound! For, where
You would hear pure, clear words outpour,*
Friar Lubin is never there.

        Envoi
   For naught but vice and sin galore,
Friar Lubin is there therefor;
But for deeds virtuous, best beware!
Friar Lubin is never there.

                          Ballades, III

*Marot's allusion here is rather obscure. I offer a translation that, if not exact, preserves the general intent, I think. [NRS]

RONDEAUX

Du mal content d'Amours

D'estre amoureux n'ay plus intention,
C'est maintenant ma moindre affection,
Car celle là, de qui je cuydoye estre
Le bien aymé, m'a bien faict apparoistre,
Qu'au faict d'amour n'y a que fiction.

Je la pensoys sans imperfection,
Mais d'aultre Amy a prins possession:
Et pource plus ne me veulx entremettre
            D'estre amoureux.

Au temps present par toute nation
Les Dames sont comme ung petit Syon,
Qui tousjours ploye à dextre, & à senestre.
Brief, les plus fins ne s'y sçavent congnoistre:
Parquoy concludz, que c'est abusion
            D'estre amoureux.★

★The rondeau takes its name from the round that was sung and danced to
in medieval entertainments. Its most frequent form is the one practiced here:
three stanzas in octosyllables or decasyllables of five, three, and five lines,
with a refrain at the end of the last two stanzas that repeats the words of the
poem's opening hemistich. Thomas Sebillet, *Art poétique* (1548), called this
form the double rondeau, and Marot was its most illustrious practitioner. Du

Of One Unhappy with Love

To be in love I have no appetite;
Nay, none whatever; none, however slight:
For she whose beau was I—or so I thought—
Has taught me well that love, though dearly sought,
Is ever false and never goes aright.

I deemed her without flaw, nor dreamed she might
Becharm another to her heart's delight!
Wherefore I warrant that no more I ought
    To be in love.

Everywhere now we see the selfsame sight:
Ladies, like reeds, sway, bend; and men, despite
Whatever they may know, indeed know naught
About their ladies' wiles and ways, ill taught:
Whence I declare, it is sheer folly, quite,
    To be in love.

Rondeaux, IX

Bellay later disdains "fixed form" poems, calling them *épiceries* (spices) that spoil the taste of the French language (*Deffense et illustration de la langue françoyse*, 1549). [HG]

De l'Amant doloreux

Avant mes jours mort me fault encourir
Par un regard, dont m'as voulu ferir,
Et ne te chault de ma griefve tristesse:
Mais n'est ce pas à toy grande rudesse,
Veu que tu peulx si bien me secourir?

Aupres de l'eau me fault de soif perir,★
Je me voy jeune, & en aage fleurir,
Et si me monstre estre plein de vieillesse
        Avant mes jours.

Or si je meurs, je veulx Dieu requerir
Prendre mon ame: & sans plus enquerir,
Je donne aux vers mon Corps plein de foiblesse.
Quant est du Cueur, du tout je le te laisse,
Ce nonobstant que me fasses mourir
        Avant mes jours.

★It is not unlikely that Marot was recalling here the already proverbial opening line from Ballade XXXIV of Charles d'Orléans (1391–1465): "Je meurs de soif auprès de la fontaine" (I die of thirst though by the stream I lie). [NRS]

Of the Suffering Lover

Before my time I bid this life good-bye,
Pierced by a deadly glance shot from your eye.
To my distress you offer not a thought;
Why must you, who can cure my ill, do naught,
And solace to my wretchedness deny?

I die of thirst though by a stream I lie:
Yet in the flower of youth, swift my days fly,
And I grow old—far older than I ought!—
            Before my time.

Ah, if I perish, I pray God on high
Possess my soul; and, with no "how" or "why,"
I give the worms my flesh, of weakness wrought;
But, for my heart, I leave it, sorrow-fraught,
To you, though 'tis because of you I die,
            Before my time.

                        Rondeaux, XI

Du conflict en douleurs

Si j'ay du mal, maulgré moy je le porte,
Et s'ainsi est, qu'aulcun me reconforte,
Son reconfort ma douleur poinct n'appaise:
Voylà comment je languis en mal aise
Sans nul espoir de liesse plus forte.

Et fault qu'ennuy jamais de moy ne sorte,
Car mon estat fut faict de telle sorte,
Des que fuz né. Pourtant ne vous desplaise,
          Si j'ay du mal.

Quand je mourray, ma douleur sera morte,
Mais ce pendant mon pauvre cueur supporte
Mes tristes jours en Fortune maulvaise:
Dont force m'est que mon ennuy me plaise,
Et ne fault plus que je me desconforte,
          Si j'ay du mal.

Of One Surfeited with Woe

If I fare ill, yet do I bear that bane
Despite myself; though one would soothe my pain,
His comfort can, alas, not comfort me:
Thus do I languish in my misery
And every hope of cheer or joy disdain.

Never must trouble quit me, never wane,
For born was I to woe, and so remain;
Wherefore I pray you not distempered be
      If I fare ill.

My grief will die when I in death have lain;
Till then, I fear, my heavy heart would fain
Suffer the sorrows of my destiny;
Take pleasure, even, in my woe; sustain
And nourish it, nor scorn its company
      If I fare ill.

Rondeaux, XXVIII

Des Nonnes, qui sortirent du Couvent pour se aller recréer

Hors du Couvent l'autrehyer soubz la Couldrette
Je rencontray mainte Nonne proprette
Suyvant l'Abbesse en grand devotion:
Si cours apres, & par affection
Vins aborder la plus jeune, & tendrette.

Je l'arraisonne, elle plainct, & regrette,
Dont je congneus (certes) que la pauvrette
Eust bien voulu aultre vacation
            Hors du Couvent.

Toutes avoient soubz vesture secrette
Ung tainct vermeil, une mine saffrette,
Sans point avoir d'Amour fruition.
Ha (dis je lors) quelle perdition
Se faict icy de ce, dont j'ay souffrette
            Hors du Couvent.

Of Nuns, Who Went from the Convent to Go Frolic

Without the convent walls the other day,
In hazel grove, I met, passing my way,
A band of comely nuns, all piously
Behind their abbess. I, quick to make free,
Approached the tenderest and said my say.

I questioned her, and she, quick to betray
Her heart, revealed that, dared she disobey,
She would prefer a different destiny
      Without the convent walls.

Beneath the habits that concealed them, they
Were ruddy-hued, each face winsome and gay,
Though never had they known love's ecstasy.
Thought I, "Ah, what a woe is this for me:
Their loss is mine no less, mine the dismay,
      Without the convent walls."

Rondeaux, XXXVII

De sa grand Amye

Dedans Paris Ville jolye
Ung jour passant melancolie
Je prins alliance nouvelle
A la plus gaye Damoyselle,
Qui soit d'icy en Italie.

D'honnesteté elle est saisie,
Et croy (selon ma fantaisie)
Qu'il n'en est gueres de plus belle
      Dedans Paris.

Je ne la vous nommeray mye,
Si non que c'est ma grand Amye;
Car l'alliance se feit telle,
Par ung doulx baiser, que j'eus d'elle
Sans penser aulcune infamie,
      Dedans Paris.

Of His Fine Damosel

In Paris, city passing fair,
One day, deep in my dark despair,
I met a fresh young damosel,
Gayest of all who gaily dwell
'Twixt here and Italy, I swear!

Decorous, simple, debonair
Was she; nor will you, anywhere,
Find any fairer, truth to tell,
   In Paris.

Name her I'll not, but I declare
That she and I are now a pair,
Formed with a kiss; nor have I fell
Intent: I would but love her well,
And every base design forbear,
   In Paris.

Rondeaux, XXXIX

Du content en Amours

Là me tiendray, où à present me tien,
Car ma Maistresse au plaisant entretien
M'ayme d'un cueur tant bon, et desirable,
Qu'on me debvroit appeler miserable,
Si mon vouloir estoit aultre que sien.

Et fusse Helaine au gratieux maintien,
Qui me vint dire, Amy, faiz mon cueur tien,
Je respondroys, point ne seray muable:
      Là me tiendray.

Qu'un chascun donc voise chercher son bien:
Quant est de moy, je me trouve tresbien.
J'ay Dame belle, exquise, et honnorable:
Parquoy fussé je unze mil ans durable,
Au dieu d'Amours ne demanderay rien:
      Là me tiendray.

Of the Man Happy in Love

Here shall I stay, and never shall I stir;
A belle as fair as belles that ever were
Loves me with heart so pure, filled with such grace,
That one, indeed, might think me vile and base
Were I to love another more than her.

Even should noble Helen say: "Monsieur,
Here, take my heart, 'tis yours!" I should demur:
"I'll not be moved, madame! This is my place;
        Here shall I stay!"

Let others seek whatever riches spur
Them on; myself, I have what I prefer:
Milady, true of heart, winsome of face.
Could I draw out my days, aeons apace,
None could I ask of Cupid comelier.
        Here shall I stay!

Rondeaux, XLVII

De celluy, qui ne pense qu'en s'Amye★

Toutes les nuictz je ne pense qu'en celle,
Qui a le Corps plus gent qu'une pucelle
De quatorze ans, sur le poinct d'enrager,
Et au dedans ung cueur (pour abreger)
Autant joyeulx qu'eut oncque Damoyselle.

Elle a beau tainct, ung parler de bon zelle,
Et le Tetin rond comme une Grozelle.
N'ay je donc pas bien cause de songer
Toutes les nuictz?

Touchant son cueur, je l'ay en ma cordelle,
Et son Mary n'a sinon le Corps d'elle:†
Mais toutesfois, quand il vouldra changer,
Prenne le Cueur: et pour le soulager
J'auray pour moy le gent Corps de la belle
Toutes les nuictz.

★The adjective-noun combination "s'Amye," an elision of the feminine "sa Amye," reflects the Middle French construction that has not yet moved to an aurally more sonorous linking assured by a consonant preceding the initial vowel of the noun. The phonetic shift to the seemingly illogical use of the masculine "son" occurred in the 1540s. [HG]

†The *rime équivoquée* (equivocal or ambiguous rhyme) of "cordelle" with "Corps d'elle" becomes a pun when it extends over multiple words. Play with homonyms was raised to an art by the school of poets called the Grands Rhétoriqueurs (among whom were Jean Molinet and the poet's own father, Jean Marot), who greatly influenced Marot's early experiments with wordplay. [HG]

Of One Who Thinks But of His Wench

Night after night, unceasing have I lain,
With thoughts of her alone haunting my brain.
Her flesh: a virgin maid's, ready to sprout
And heat to passion; and her heart: no doubt
The happiest ever in all love's domain.

What? Do you think I muse on her in vain—
Fair skin, voice full of fire, teats standing out
Like berries, currants round, and taut, and stout—
        Night after night?

Though I possess her heart, another swain,
Her husband (fie!) it is—need I explain?—
Who has her body. Ah, if but the lout
Would trade, how I would greet the turnabout:
That body, mine beneath the counterpane,
        Night after night!

Rondeaux, XLV

CHANSONS

Je suis aymé de la plus belle,
Qui soit vivant dessoubz les Cieulx:
Encontre tous faulx Envieulx
Je la soustiendray estre telle.

Si Cupido doulx, et rebelle
Avoit desbendé ses deux yeux,
Pour veoir son maintien gracieux,
Je croy qu'amoureux seroit d'elle.

Venus la Deesse immortelle
Tu as faict mon cueur bien heureux,
De l'avoir faict estre amoureux
D'une si noble Damoyselle.

The fairest of the fair loves me;
Let jealous mortals mock my choice,
I shall repeat with eager voice:
Of all the fair, the fairest she.

Would knavish Cupid but untie
The band about his eyes, and see
Her graceful air, I think that he
Would love her quite as much as I.

Venus, indeed you treat me well,
For with divine, undying art
You have inspired my happy heart
With love of noble damosel.

Chansons, X

Mauldicte soit la mondaine richesse,
Qui m'a osté m'Amye, et ma Maistresse.★
Las par vertu j'ay son amytié quise,
Mais par richesse ung aultre l'a conquise:
Vertu n'a pas en amour grand prouesse.

Dieu gard de mal la Nymphe, et la Deesse:
Mauldict soit l'Or, où elle a sa liesse,
Mauldicte soit la fine Soye exquise,
Le Dyamant, et la Perle requise
Puis que par eulx il fault qu'elle me laisse.

★See comments on "s'Amye," p. 38, note. Interestingly, the Middle French combination "m'amye," often written as "ma mie," is the origin of the English given name "Mamie," just as "ma belle" is the source of "Mabel." [NRS]

A curse on wealth, for it has snatched from me
Milady, mistress mine. Though honestly
And loyally I wooed, yet welladay!
Another's wealth has stolen her away:
Love pays no high esteem to loyalty.

Goddess and nymph, I pray God spare the belle,
But may He cast her riches into Hell:
Cursed be the silks, the pearl, the diamond bright,
Cursed be the gold, object of her delight;
To them alone I owe her cruel farewell.

Chansons, XIX

Qui veult entrer en grâce
Des Dames bien avant,
En cautelle, & fallace
Fault estre bien sçavant.
Car tout vray Poursuyvant,
La loyaulté suyvant,
Au jourd'huy est deceu:
Et le plus decepvant
Pour loyal est receu.

He who desires to dwell
In lady's heart, and reign
Therein, must learn full well
To cozen and chicane:
For true and loyal swain
Pays court today in vain
If loyal be his suit;
Whilst he who learns to feign
Is held in high repute.

Chansons, XXII

D'Amours me va tout au rebours,
Jà ne fault, que de cela mente,
J'ay reffus en lieu de secours:
M'amye rit, & je lamente.
C'est la cause pourquoy je chante,
D'Amours me va tout au rebours,
Tout au rebours me va d'Amours.*

---

*The repetition and inversion form a chiasmus that underscores, syntac-
tically, the poem's (and lover's) impasse by turning back on itself, and on line
1. See also the poem "O Cruaulté logée en grand beaulté," p. 50, for Marot's
flair with chiasmus. [HG]

I say, love uses me awry,
Nor speak I false when I complain;
"Nay" is milady's cruel reply;
No ease she proffers for my pain.
Naught but a laugh; hence my refrain:
"I say, love uses me awry,
Awry love uses me, say I."

Chansons, XXVII

    J'ay grand desir
D'avoir plaisir
D'amour mondaine:
Mais c'est grand peine,
Car chascun loyal amoureux
Au temps present est malheureux:
Et le plus fin
Gaigne à la fin
La grâce pleine.

Oh, how I yearn,
In vain, to earn
Love's worldly pleasure!
Woe beyond measure
Is all my lot; for lover true,
Today, earns not true lover's due:
None but who use
Wit, wile, and ruse
Win love's fair treasure.

Chansons, XXVIII

O Cruaulté logée en grand beaulté,
O grand beaulté, qui loges cruaulté,
Quand ma douleur jamais ne sentiras,
Au moins ung jour pense en ma loyaulté:
Ingrate alors (peult estre) te diras.

O beauty, where dwells cruel hard-heartedness,
O hard heart, where dwells beauty nonetheless.
One day, at least, muse on my loyalty,
Though never will you feel my woe! Ah yes,
Then might you think: "How thankless I could be!"

Chansons, **XXIX**

La plus belle des troys sera
Celle, qui mourir me fera,
Ou qui me fera du tout vivre,
Car de mon mal seray delivre,
Quand à sa puissance plaira.

Pallas point ne m'aidera:
Juno point ne s'en meslera:
Mais Venus, que j'ay voulu suivre,
Me dira bien, tien je te livre
Celle, qui ravy ton cueur a.

She who must be the death of me,
Or who must let me live, of three
Goddesses is the comeliest;
For I, by love's travail possessed,
Might, at her pleasure, succored be.

Pallas will spurn my plaint, my plea;
Juno will scorn my woe; but she,
Venus, whom I above the rest
Have served, will say: "Here, heart distressed,
Take her who whets your agony."

Chansons, XXXIII

Puis que de vous je n'ay aultre visage,
Je m'en vois rendre hermite en ung desert,
Pour prier dieu, si ung aultre vous sert,
Qu'aultant que moy en vostre honneur soit sage.

A dieu Amours, à dieu gentil corsage,
A dieu ce tainct, à dieu ces frians yeux:
Je n'ay pas heu de vous grand adventage:
Ung moins aymant aura, peult estre, mieulx.

Since with your favor I may not be blessed,
A hermit in the desert shall I be,
To pray that he who serves you after me
Preserve your honor in his amorous quest.

Good-bye to love, good-bye sweet, tender breast,
Good-bye fair skin, enticing eyes, good-bye!
I had but little use of you at best;
Who loves you less may use you more than I.

Chansons, XXXIV

Vous perdez temps de me dire mal d'elle,
Gens qui voulez divertir mon entente:
Plus la blasmez, plus je la trouve belle.
S'esbahist on, si tant je m'en contente?
La fleur de sa jeunesse
A vostre advis rien n'est ce?
N'est ce rien que ses grâces?
Cessez voz grands audaces,
Car mon Amour vaincra vostre mesdire:
Tel en mesdict, qui pour soy la desire.

You waste your time jabbering ill of her,
You, who my choice are ever criticizing:
The more you vilify, the lovelier
I find her; why deem you my love surprising?
Count you for naught her face's,
Her body's youthful graces,
A-bloom with tendernesses?
Enough, your bold excesses!
My love will thwart your slurs ignobly sown:
Who slurs her doubtless wants her for his own.

Chansons, XXXV

Ne sçay combien la hayne est dure,
Et n'ay desir de le sçavoir:
Mais je sçay qu'amour, qui peu dure,★
Faict ung grand tourment recepvoir.
Amour aultre nom deust avoir,
Nommer la fault Fleur, ou Verdure,
Qui peu de temps se laisse veoir.

Nommer le donc Fleur, ou Verdure
Au cueur de mon legier Amant:
Mais en mon cueur, qui trop endure,
Nommez le Roc, ou Dyamant,
Car je vy tousjours en aymant,
En aymant celluy qui procure,†
Que Mort me voyse consommant.

★The equivocal rhyme "dure/dure" plays on words that have the same
sound and different meanings. [HG]
   †Given the masculine gender of "legier Amant" and "celluy," the poetic
voice of this chanson both lamenting love's inconsistency on one hand and
praising its constancy on the other seems, uncharacteristically, to be that of
the female. [NRS]

I know not how hard hate may be,
Nor wish to know so, I confess;
But love, which passes fleetingly,
I know, can cause much sore distress.
Love ought some other name possess:
Give the name "flower," or "greenery,"
For these live little, even less.

Yes, name it "flower," or "greenery,"
When in the heart of my gallant;
But I, who live long agony,
Ought name mine "rock," or "adamant":
For, in my heart, no fragile plant
Is love: long love I faithfully
Who respite from Death's grip can grant.

Chansons, XL

Mon cueur se recommande à vous,
Tout plein d'Ennuy, et de Martire:
Au moins en despit des Jaloux
Faictes qu'à Dieu vous puisse dire.
Ma bouche, qui vous souloit rire,
Et compter propos gracieux,
Ne faict maintenant que mauldire
Ceulx, qui m'ont banny de voz yeux.

Banny j'en suis par faulx semblant:
Mais pour nous veoir encor ensemble,
Fault que me soiez ressemblant
De fermeté: car il me semble
Que quand faulx Rapport desassemble
Les Amans, qui sont assemblez,
Si ferme amour ne les r'assemble
Sans fin seront desassemblez.

My heart commends itself to you,
Full to the brim with sorrows fell;
Despite what jealous folk may do,
Let me, at least, sigh my farewell.
My lips, that pleasantries would tell,
Now only curse those knaves whose spite
Has cast me from where I would dwell,
Evermore in your tender sight.

Cast out am I by False Pretense;★
But if we once again would be
Rejoined, then from this moment hence
Be strong, like me; for certainly
When False Report works villainy
Against two lovers bound together,
Unless Strong Love rejoin them, he
Shall have forever cut their tether.

Chansons, XLII

★The reader will recognize the allegorical figures inherited from the thirteenth-century two-part poem *Le Roman de la Rose,* of Guillaume de Lorris and Jean de Meung, influential throughout the Middle Ages and beyond, an edition of which Marot himself prepared in 1524. [NRS]

ELEGIES

La grand Amour, que mon las cueur vous porte,
Incessamment me conseille, & enhorte
Vous consoller en vostre ennuy extrême:
Mais (tout bien veu) je treuve que moymesme
Ay bon besoing de consolation
Du dueil, que j'ay de vostre affliction.
J'en ay tel dueil qu'a peine eusse sceu mettre
Sur le papier ung tout seul petit Metre,
Si le desir, qu'ay à vostre service,
N'eust esté grand, et plein d'amour sans vice.

Ô Dieu du Ciel, qu'amour est forte chose.
Sept ans y a que ma main se repose
Sans voulenté d'escrire à nulle femme,
M'eust elle aymé soubz tresardante flamme:
Et maintenant (las) une Damoyselle
Qui n'a sur moy affection, ne zelle,
Me faict pour elle employer Encre, et Plume,
Et sans m'aymer, d'un feu nouveau m'allume.

Or me traictez ainsi qu'il vous plaira:
En endurant mon cueur vous servira:
Et ayme mieulx vous servir en tristesse,
Qu'aymer ailleurs en joye, et en lyesse.

The love that my heart, in its weariness,
Bears at your grief, exhorts me to express
My consolation; though I feel, indeed,
Such woe at your distress that I, in need
No less of pity than yourself, *ma chère,*
Lament your pain and my own deep despair.
Yes, such my woe that I could not have written
One single verse if I had not been smitten,
Utterly, by a pure, unblemished love,
And by the wish to serve you, born thereof.

O God in heaven, alas! How strong a thing
Is love! For seven years, stilled, languishing,
My hand, unquilled, unwilling, would not write
To any woman, even one who might
Have loved me with a burning flame: yet now,
A maid unfeeling, cold—alas!—somehow
Makes me, unloved, take up my ink and pen,
And, loving not, fills me with fire again.

Wherefore I say, do with me what you will:
My heart, the while, gladly will serve you still.
Sooner would I serve you, though sore distressed,
Than elsewhere love in joy and pleasure-blessed.

D'où vient ce point? Certes il fault bien dire,
Qu'en vous y a quelcque grâce, qui tire
Les cueurs à soy. Mais laquelle peult ce estre?
Seroit ce point vostre port tant à dextre?
Seroit ce point les traictz de voz beaulx yeux,
Ou ce parler tant doulx, et gratieux?
Seroit ce point vostre bonté tant sage,
Ou la haulteur de ce tant beau corsage?
Seroit ce point vostre entiere beaulté,
Ou ceste doulce honneste privaulté?
C'est ceste là (ainsi comme il me semble)
Ou si [ne] faulx, ce sont toutes ensemble.   [je]
Quoy que ce soit, de vostre amour suis pris:
Encor je loue Amour en mes espritz,
De mon cueur mettre en ung lieu tant heureux,
Puis qu'il falloit que devinse amoureux.

   Donc puis qu'Amour m'a voulu arrester
Pour vous servir, plaise vous me traicter,
Comme vouldriez vous mesme estre traictée,
Si vous estiez par Amour arrestée.

How comes it thus to be? Doubtless because
You are of grace possessed; a force that draws
Hearts unto you. But why? What force? Perchance
It is your stately bearing? Or that glance
Darting its arrows from your eyes? Or your
Soft, graceful speech? Or is it your demure,
Gentle good manners? Or perhaps your heaving,
Firm, upturned breasts, fair bosom proudly cleaving?
Or can it be your whole being, passing fair,
Or your decorous mien and modest air?
Ah! That last it must be—or so I find—
Unless it be all of those things combined.
No matter: I lie captured by whatever
Power your loveliness possess. However,
Happily I praise Cupid; for his art
Finds me the perfect place to lodge my heart.

Thus, inasmuch as Love has chosen me
To serve you as your loyal devotee,
I pray you treat me quite as one would do
If, in like manner, Love had chosen you.

Elegies, IX★

★The elegy made its appearance in France around 1500 and bears affinities
with the medieval genre of the *complainte.* The central notion of both is the
Latin *planctus,* or regret, that follows the death of a loved one. In the mid-
sixteenth century Thomas Sebillet defined the elegy as a sad poem, most
often conveying the melancholy of love (*Art poétique*). The word is derived
from the Greek *elegos* (plaint). [HG]

Amour me feit escrire au Moys de May
Nouveau refrain, par lequel vous nommay
(Comme sçavez) la plus belle de France:
Mais je failly, car veu la souffisance
De la beaulté, qui dessus vous abonde,
Dire debvois, la plus belle du Monde:
Ce qui en est, & qu'on en voit, m'accuse
De telle faulte, et vostre amour m'excuse,
Qui troubla tant mes doloreux espritz,
Que France alors pour le Monde je pris.

O doncques vous du Monde la plus belle,
Ne cachez pas ung cueur dur, & rebelle
Soubz tel beaulté: ce seroit grand dommage:
Mais à mon cueur, qui vous vient faire hommage,
Faictes recueil: je vous en fais present,
Voyez le bien, il est (certes) exempt
De faulx Penser, Fainctise, ou Trahison,
Il n'a sur luy faulte, ne mesprison,
En luy ne sont aulcunes amours vaines,
Tout ce qu'il a de maulvais, ce sont peines,
Qui de par vous y ont este boutées,
Et qui sans vous n'en peulvent estre ostées.

Si vous supply, m'Amye, & mon recours,
Belle, en qui gist ma mort, ou mon secours,
Prenez mon cueur, que je vous viens offrir,
Et s'il est faulx, faictes le bien souffrir,
Mais s'il est bon, & de loyalle sorte,
Arrachez luy tant de peines, qu'il porte.

Love bade me write, in May, a springtime song
To sing your beauty, but I sang it wrong:
For, as you know, I called you the most fair
In all of France, instead of everywhere.
"France" did I say, "the world" was what I meant,
Such is your beauty; and yet, innocent
Of fault am I, for love of you did so
Confound my spirit and compound my woe,
That, all askew of mind and wits askance,
Although I thought "the world" my pen wrote "France."

Thus do I beg that you who are, indeed,
In all the world the fairest, feel no need
To let your beauty mask, revengefully,
A heart of stone: great pity would that be.
Rather, I pray you welcome mine, for it
Bears homage most sincere, with never a whit
Of fraud, or feint, or traitorous pretense;
With naught of evil in it but what you
Yourself have caused: to wit, the agonies
That you have wrought, and you alone can ease.

And so, sweet refuge and most beauteous friend,
You who have power to succor me or end
My life, I beg you take this heart of mine.
If it be false, then let it languish, pine,
And suffer; but if loyal, hear my prayer:
Strip it free of its anguish and despair.

Elegies, XI

EPISTRES

Marot à Monseigneur Bouchart Docteur en Theologie

Donne response à mon present affaire,
Docte docteur. Qui t'a induict à faire
Emprisonner depuis six jours en ça
Ung tien amy, qui onc ne t'offensa?
Et vouloir mettre en luy crainte, & terreur
D'aigre justice, en disant que l'erreur
Tiens de Luther? Point ne suis Lutheriste,★
Ne Zvinglien, & moins Anabatiste:
[Sinon de] Dieu par son filz Jesuchrist.   [Je suis]

★See also the *epistre* "Au Roi, du temps de son exil à Ferrare" (1535 or 1536), in which the poet denies rumors that he is a Lutheran: "De Luthériste ils m'ont donné le nom; / Qu'à droit ce soit, je leur réponds que non" (They have called me a Lutheran / To which let me rightly tell them no) (2:87–88). The accusations leading to Marot's imprisonment in 1526 were revived in March 1532. In the later poem Marot employs the same strategy as in the present one; that is, to affirm that he is baptized in the name of Christ. By the date of the Ferrara poem, however, that assertion had become dangerous, since the theologians of the Sorbonne had excluded the formula "au nom du Pere, Fils, et Saint Esprit" from the baptism ritual. Marot's self-defense thus carried an ironic counterattack against the church establishment. [HG]

Marot to Monseigneur Bouchart, Doctor of Theology

   Offer me, pray, in my fell situation—
Doctor doctrinal, wise—some explanation:
Who has persuaded you to see to it
That I, your friend, who never, not one whit,
Did you the slightest ill, should, these days six,
Be prisoned, claiming that the heretics'
Foul sins are mine as well, and I must be,
By a harsh justice, punished fearsomely?
Nor Luther's creed, nor Zwingli's I profess,
And—'sdeath!—the Anabaptists' even less!
God's alone am I, by the Christ, his son.

Je suis celluy, qui ay faict mainst escript,
Dont ung seul vers on n'en sçauroit extraire,
Qui à la Loy divine soit contraire.
Je suis celuy, qui prends plaisir, & peine
A louer Christ, & sa Mere tant pleine
De grâce infuse: & pour bien l'esprouver,
On le pourra par mes escriptz trouver.

Brief, celluy suis, qui croit, honnore, & prise
La saincte, vraie, & catholique Eglise.★
Aultre doctrine en moy ne veulx bouter:
Ma Loy est bonne. Et si ne fault doubter,
Qu'à mon pouvoir ne la prise, & exaulce,
Veu qu'ung Payen prise la sienne faulse.
Que quiers tu donc, ô Docteur catholique?
Que quiers tu donc? As tu aulcune picque
Encontre moy? ou si tu prends saveur
A me trister dessoubz aultruy faveur?

Je croy que non: mais quelcque faulx entendre
T'a faict sur moy telle rigueur estendre.
Doncques refrains de ton couraige l'ire.
Que pleust à Dieu, qu'ores tu peusses lire
Dedans ce corps de franchise interdit,
Le cueur verrois aultre qu'on ne t'a dit.

A tant me tais, cher Seigneur nostre Maistre,
Te suppliant, à ce coup amy m'estre.
Et si pour moy à raison tu n'es mis,
Fais quelcque chose au moins pour mes amys,
En me rendant par une horsboutée
La liberté, laquelle m'as ostée.

★The "catholique Eglise" that Marot claims as his own is, of course, the
church universal, not the Catholic Church of Rome. [HG]

I am he, in whose myriad verses, none,
Not one is there false to his Law divine.
I am he, who, in joy, strive to make shine
His name, and praise his Mother, full of grace!
Let doubters read my works. I rest my case.

In short, I am he, who does every due
Homage unto the one and only true
Catholic Church! No lesser Law within
My heart was, is, nor has one ever been.
Why think you so? Why? If a Heathen base
Reveres his false faith, should not I embrace
The truth with all the power and might I may?
What would you, then, O Catholic sage, I pray?
What would you, then? Have you some grief, some plaint
Against me? Or take you some pleasure quaint
Burdening me beneath more dole, and woe,
And pain than you toward other men would show?

No, you could not! Thus do I beg you, please—
Whoever might have spread such villainies
About me—let your heart's ire not be stirred
By falsehood that, no doubt, from such you heard.
God willing, may you read in this flesh, penned,
A purer heart than lying tongues pretend.

So, Sire and Master, shall I say no more:
Be not to this a party, I implore.
If you be not for me myself inclined
To reason, then, pray to my friends be kind:
Come, kick me out unceremoniously,
Back to the freedom that you took from me.

Epistres, X★

★The present *epistre* and the next one are two of eleven such early works
presented under the heading *L'Adolescence clémentine* (*Clément's Youth*), as
opposed to the group of thirty somewhat later examples of the genre, of
more varied form and inspiration, from which our third and fourth *epistres*
(pp. 80–83) are taken. (See Defaux 1:91–94, 327.) [NRS]

Epistre à son amy Lyon

Je ne t'escry de l'amour vaine, & folle,
Tu voys assez, s'elle sert, ou affolle:
Je ne t'escry ne d'Armes, ne de Guerre,
Tu voys, qui peult bien, ou mal y acquerre:
Je ne t'escry de Fortune puissante,
Tu voys assez, s'elle est ferme, ou glissante:
Je ne t'escry d'abus trop abusant,
Tu en sçais prou, & si n'en vas usant:
Je ne t'escry de Dieu, ne sa puissance,
C'est a luy seul t'en donner congnoissance:
Je ne t'escry des Dames de Paris,
Tu en sçais plus que leurs propres Maris:
Je ne t'escry, qui est rude, ou affable,
Mais je te veulx dire une belle fable:
C'est assavoir du Lyon, & du Rat.

Cestuy Lyon plus fort qu'un vieulx Verrat,
Veit une fois, que le Rat ne sçavoit
Sortir d'ung lieu, pour autant qu'il avoit
Mangé le lard, & la chair toute crue:★
Mais ce Lyon (qui jamais ne fut Grue)
Trouva moyen, & maniere, & matiere
D'ongles, & dentz, de rompre la ratiere:
Dont maistre rat eschappe vistement:

★Marot landed in the Châtelet prison in 1526 as a result of accusations of
Lutheranism, but legend had it that he had been accused of breaking the
Lenten fast by eating meat, as is implied here. The latter reading clearly
suggests that the present *epistre* is autobiographical; and it is indeed the case
that Lion (or Léon) Jamet was a close friend, who would flee France, as
Marot himself would do, following the Affaire des Placards in 1534. On the
other hand, the reference to lard-eating need not be taken as proof, since the
expression *manger le lard* had been used since the Middle Ages simply to mean
"to be a thief." [HG]

Epistle to His Friend Lyon

   I write you not of love, foolish and vain,
You know full well its pleasure and its pain;
I write you not of war or feats of arms,
You know the bane they offer, and the charms;
I write you not of mighty Destiny,
You know how firm or fickle she can be;
I write you not of wrongs and ills ill-wrought,
You know them all, I vow, though you sin not;
I write you not of God's power infinite,
He alone ought make you aware of it;
I write you not of Paris ladies, you
Who know more of them than their husbands do;
I write you not of manners, fine or fell,
But rather would a simple fable tell:
The tale about the Lion and the Rat.

   Strong as a tough old boar—stronger, at that—
A Lion, once upon a time, observed
A Rat, caught tight, grown fat from having served
Himself great quantities of lard and meat
Uncooked; who, eating what one should not eat,
Could not escape the trap, hard though he try.
But Lion—not one to stand idly by,
Cranelike—by hook and crook (claws, fangs, that is),
Was able, with that strength and skill of his,
To rip the trap; whereat Sire Rat, set free,

Puis mist à terre ung genoul gentement,
Et en ostant son bonnet de la teste,
A mercié mille fois la grant Beste:
Jurant le dieu des Souriz, et des Ratz,
Qu'il luy rendroit. Maintenant tu verras
Le bon du compte. Il advint d'adventure,
Que le Lyon pour chercher sa pasture,
Saillit dehors sa caverne, & son siege:
Dont (par malheur) se trouva pris au piege,
Et fut lié contre un ferme posteau.

    Adonc le Rat, sans serpe, ne cousteau,
Y arriva joyeulx, & esbaudy,
Et du Lyon (pour vray) ne s'est gaudy:
Mais despita Chatz, Chates, & Chatons,
Et prisa fort Ratz, Rates, & Ratons,
Dont il avoit trouvé temps favorable
Pour secourir le Lyon secourable:
Auquel a dit: tays toy Lyon lié,
Par moy seras maintenant deslié:
Tu le vaulx bien, car le cueur joly as.
Bien y parut, quand tu me deslias.
Secouru m'as fort Lyonneusement,
Ors secouru seras Rateusement.

Kneels down before him and, most courteously
Doffing his bonnet, offers thanks galore
(At least a thousand) to the beast; what's more,
He swears by that good god who rules the fate
Of rat and mouse that, if reciprocate
He might, most surely will he do so. Well,
Now comes the best part of this tale I tell.
It came to pass that Lion, from his lair
Set out one day to graze the field. But there,
Suddenly, he lay trapped, alas! and bound
Tight to a stake stuck firmly in the ground.

    Whereupon, as it happened, empty-pawed
But gaily tripping as he trod abroad,
Round came our Rat; he took no joy, for sure,
To see the Lion's sad discomfiture.
He scorned all cats and catlets, great and small,
Esteeming rats and ratlets, one and all.
Yet did he find the time was ripe, behaving
Kindly to one so much in need of saving.
Whence: "Hush, good Lion, lying bound, distraught.
Now shall you be by me set free, uncaught!
Your noble heart you showed me, Lion-wise:
My favor now your good deed Ratifies."

Lors le Lyon ses deux grands yeux vestit,
Et vers le Rat les tourna ung petit,
En luy disant, ô pauvre vermyniere,
Tu n'as sur toy instrument, ne maniere,
Tu n'as cousteau, serpe, ne serpillon,
Qui sceut coupper corde, ne cordillon,
Pour me getter de ceste estroicte voye;
Va te cacher, que le Chat ne te voye.

Sire Lyon (dit le filz de Souris)
De ton propos (certes) je me soubris:
J'ay des cousteaulx assez, ne te soucie,
De bel os blanc plus tranchant qu'une Cye:
Leur gaine c'est ma gencive, & ma bouche:
Bien coupperont la corde, qui te touche
De si trespres: car j'y mettray bon ordre.

Lors Sire Rat va commencer à mordre
Ce gros lien: vray est qu'il y songea
Assez long temps: mais il le vous rongea
Souvent & tant, qu'à la parfin tout rompt:
Et le Lyon de s'en aller fut prompt,
Disant en soy: nul plaisir (en effect)
Ne se perdt point, quelcque part où soit faict.
Voylà le compte en termes rimassez:
Il est bien long: mais il est vieil assez,
Tesmoing Esope, & plus d'ung million.*

*Marot lets his enthusiasm slightly get the better of him. Although the
fable does indeed go back to Aesop, and although many later fabulists did
subsequent versions of it, his "ung million" is, of course, a trifle exaggerated.
The best known of the versions is probably that of La Fontaine, in his *Fables*
(2:11). (For my translation, see my *Fifty More Fables of La Fontaine* [Urbana:
University of Illinois Press, 1998], p. 21.) Gérard Defaux, in a note to the
present text, cites an article by Jacques Berthold that attributes to Marot's
celebrated version a philosophico-aesthetic subject: the freeing of poetic
language from the straitjacket of rhetoric. (See Defaux 1:478.) [NRS]

Eyes dimmed, the Lion turned his head a bit,
Casting a look of tender doubt. "Poor nit,"
He said. "My worm-infested friend, tut tut!
You think that you can save me? Well, with what?
You have no knife, no crook, no hook... In fact,
Nothing to cut the merest thread: intact
Will be my bonds, despite you, I'll be bound!
Best you go hide lest soon the cat come round!"

    "Sire," says the scion of the mousely race,
"What you say puts a smile upon my face.
See? I have knives a-plenty—never doubt it—
Wrought of white bone, saw-sharp, no doubt about it!
Their scabbards are these gums, within my lips.
Here a bite, there a bite, some well-aimed snips,
And, though your bonds bind tight, soon will they fall."

    Straightway Sire Rat begins. The task, withal,
Gives him more trouble than he bargained for.
But he persists, gnaws, nibbles more and more,
Until, at length, the knots give, the cord breaks;
Whereat the grateful Lion promptly takes
His leave, reflecting to himself: "No pleasant
Deed that one does is lost." As for the present
Fable, though long, it goes far back in time:
Aesop (and millions) have turned it to rhyme.

Or viens me veoir, pour faire le Lyon:
Et je mettray peine, sens, & estude
D'estre le Rat, exempt d'ingratitude:
J'entends, si Dieu te donne autant d'affaire,
Qu'au grand Lyon: ce qu'il ne vueille faire.

   Dear friend, I pray you visit me and play
The Lion's role, freeing me how you may.
I will do all I can to play the Rat,
Grateful, and ready to give tit for tat,
But praying that I never have to do,
And that God not cast Lion's lot on you.

Epistres, XI

A mon Seigneur de Guise passant par Paris★

Va tost Epistre, il est venu, il passe,
Et part demain, des Princes l'outrepasse:
Il le te fault saluer humblement,
Et dire ainsi: Vostre humble Serf Clement
(Prince de pris) luy mesme fust venu,
Mais Maladie au Lict l'a retenu
Si longuement, qu'oncques ne fut si mince,
Pasle, et deffaict. Vray est (illustre Prince)
Qu'en ce corps mesgre est l'esprit demouré,
Qui aultrefoys a pour vous labouré,†
Non bien sachant, combien il y doit estre:
Parquoy tandis, qu'il vit en ce bas estre,
Servez vous en. Ainsi diras Epistre
A cil, qui est digne de Royal tiltre:
Puis te tairas, car tant debile suis,
Que d'ung seul vers alonger ne te puis.

★The reference is to Claude de Lorraine (1496–1550), duc de Guise, the first to bear that title, and a faithful ally of François I in his conflict with the emperor Charles V. [NRS]

†History appears not to have recorded the services to the duke to which Marot alludes, at least according to the critical edition of *Les Epîtres* by C. A. Mayer (London: Athlone, 1958, p. 181), as well as to the note in Defaux 1:729. [NRS]

To Monseigneur de Guise, Passing Through Paris

    Go, fly, epistle mine! Hither has come
The princeliest prince in all of Christendom!
Nor bides he long, for he will only stay
Until the morrow. Fly to him and say,
In humblest wise: "O gracious Majesty,
Clément, your lowly servant, begs to be
Excused for not, himself, appearing here.
Long has he lain abed, more ill, I fear—
Pale, frail, and wan—than ever has he been.
But true it is, O noble sire: within
His wizened frame remains the mind, still strong,
That served you well, though knows he not how long!
Wherefore do with it what you will." Speak thus
To *Monseigneur,* the grand and glorious,
Then say no more; for I am much too weak
To write yet one more line for you to speak.

                           Epistres, XXIII

Au Roy, pour la Bazoche★

Pour implorer vostre digne puissance,
Devers vous, Syre, en toute obeyssance
Bazochiens à ce coup sont venuz
Vous supplier d'ouyr par les menuz
Les poinctz, & traictz de nostre Comedie.
Et s'il y a rien qui picque ou mesdie,
A vostre gré l'aigreur adoulcirons.
Mais à quel juge est ce, que nous irons
Si n'est à vous? qui de toute science
Avez certaine & vraye experience,
Et qui tout seul d'authorité povez
Nous dire: Enfans, Je veulx que vous jouez.

O Syre, donc, plaise vous nous permettre
Sur le theâtre, à ce coup, nous mettre,
En conservant noz libertez & droicts,
Comme jadis feirent les autres Roys.
Si vous tiendra pour pere la Bazoche,
Qui ose bien vous dire sans reproche,
Que de tant plus son regne fleurira,
Vostre Paris tant plus resplendira.

★Regarding the authenticity of this piece, see Defaux 2:950. The "Clercs de la Basoche" (or Bazoche), originally a confraternity of legal functionaries, was a dramatic troupe dating from the Middle Ages and of great importance in the development of the medieval French comic theater. Its satiric commentaries on current events, often pushed to extremes, more than once brought official wrath down upon its head. Contrasting with the previous *epistre,* this one displays Marot's celebrated badinage in a theatrical context, thus tapping its potential as dialogue. [NRS]

To the King, for "La Basoche"

Before your royal, mighty Majesty,
Humble players of "la Basoche" come we
To beg you, Sire, to lend an ear to all
Our banter and our comic folderol.
And, should you find in what we say and do
Anything that offends or nettles you,
Willingly would we choose to alter it.
What finer judge is there, of keener wit,
Wisdom, experience, to whom we might
Appeal? Who else can give our troupe the right
To ply our craft in peace? Who else can say:
"My sons, it is my wish that you should play"?

Sire, we beseech, implore you to allow
Your servants of the theater, here and now,
Freely, and with the leave that other kings
Have granted, to perform our offerings.
Thus know we that Your Majesty will be,
Surely, the father of our *confrérie*,
And dare state that, thereby, your reign transcendent
Will see a Paris ever more resplendent.

Epistres, XXXI

CHANTS DIVERS

Cantique sur la maladie de s'Amie

Dieu, qui vouluz le plus hault ciel laisser,
Et ta haultesse en la terre abbaisser,
Là où santé donnas à maints, & maintes,
Vueilles ouyr de toutes mes complaintes
Une sans plus. Vueilles donner santé
A celle là, par qui suis tourmenté.

Ta saincte voix en l'Evangile crie,
Que tout vivant pour ses ennemys prie:
Guerys doncq celle (ô medecin parfaict)
Qui m'est contraire, & malade me faict.

Helas Seigneur: il semble, tant est belle,
Que plaisir prins à la composer telle.
Ne souffre pas advenir cest oultrage,
Que maladie efface ton ouvrage.

Son embonpoinct commence à se passer,
Jà ce beau traict se prent à effacer,

Hymn on the Illness of His Lady

O God, who chose to quit the heavenly heights
And join the mortal sphere; who put to rights
Legions of suffering souls and cured straightway
Their earthly ills; to you I humbly pray
You grant one last entreaty! Please restore
To health the lady whom I anguish for.

The Gospel, in your sacred voice, decrees
That each of us pray for our enemies;
Thus, doctor without peer, I pray you cure
My foe, cause of the ills I must endure.

Alas, such beauty did your hand confer
Upon her that, no doubt, you took in her
Great pleasure; Lord, let not disease thus wreak
Destruction on your work, matchless, unique.

Already I can see her flesh grow thin;
Her comely hue grow pallid, and begin

Et ces beaulx yeulx, clers & resplendissants,
Qui m'ont navré, deviennent languissants.★

 Il est bien vray que ceste grand' beauté
A desservy pour sa grand' cruaulté
Punition. Mais, Sire, à l'advenir
Elle pourra plus doulce devenir.

 Pardonne luy, & fais que maladie
N'ayt point l'honneur de la faire enlaydie.
Assez à temps viendra vieillesse palle,
Qui de ce faire a charge principalle:

 Et cependant si tu la maintiens saine,
Ceulx qui voyrront sa beaulté souveraine
Beneiront toy, & ta fille Nature,
D'avoir formé si belle creature:

 Et de ma part feray ung beau Cantique,
Qui chantera le miracle autentique
Que faict auras, admirable à chascun,
D'en guerir deux en n'en guerissant qu'ung.

 Non que pour moy je leve au Ciel la face,
Ne que pour moy priere je te face:
Car je te doy supplier pour son bien,
Et je la doy requerir pour le mien.

★Ill health causes his Lady's eye to dim, thus sparing the poet the pain that emanates, since Petrarch, from the eyes' deadly glance. Marot deftly fuses two voices in this poem: those of Petrarchan love and evangelical grace, the latter pleading ironically to restore his lover's power to torment him. [HG]

To fade; and in her eyes, once bright aglow,
Teasing me on, naught but her languors' woe.

True, this great beauty was so cruel that she
Deserved chastisement for her cruelty;
But in the future, Lord, one well might find
In her the best of gentle womankind.

Pardon her, pray, and let not illness own
The pride of turning her an ugly crone.
Ashen old age, in time, will loll and lurk
About, and bear the burden of that work.

Till then, if you restore her health, those who
Behold such form and feature will bless you
And Nature too, your daughter, who have wrought
A creature rare indeed, second to naught.

And I, for my part, will a paean raise
To laud your miracle and sing your praise:
The true, miraculous phenomenon
Of curing two by curing only one.

Not that I lift my eyes to heaven, upreaching
In solemn prayer, for my own self beseeching;
No: I must pray to you to make her whole,
That I may pray to her to soothe my soul.

Chants divers, X

EPIGRAMMES

A Maistre Grenoille, poëte ignorant★

Bien ressembles à la Grenoille,
Non pas que tu soys aquatique:
Mais comme en l'eau elle barbouille,
Si fays tu en l'Art Poëtique.

★This epigram, typical of most of the many written by Marot, reminds us that the form, as practiced by the Latin poets Catullus and Martial, is characterized by its brevity and its wit, the latter delivered with a sharp satirical bite. Later, in 1561, J. C. Scaliger would write that the pointed character of the epigram is its soul and that its brevity is a property that follows necessarily. [HG]

For Master Grenoille, Ignorant Poet

Indeed, you do seem quite the frog,
Though not a water beast you be:
Whilst he goes mucking through the bog,★
You muck about in poetry.

Epigrammes, I, xviii

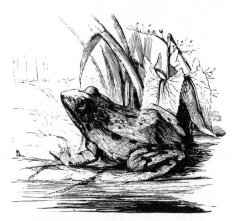

★The reader of this quatrain (whose specific referent is unknown) will
recall that, as with many animals, the grammatical gender of the French *la
grenouille* (frog) implies nothing as to its sex; hence my use of the masculine
pronoun. [NRS]

De la statue de Venus endormye

Qui dort icy? le fault il demander?
Venus y dort, qui vous peult commander.
Ne l'esveillez, elle ne vous nuyra.
Si l'esveillez, croyrez qu'elle ouvrira
Ses deux beaulx yeulx, pour les vostres bander.★

★Marot's last word, "bander" (to blindfold), also means "to have an erec-
tion," a play on words certain to amuse the reader of his day. The wordplay
cannot have been involuntary, for Marot displays throughout his work both
whimsy and skill with the spoken language. [HG]

Of the Statue of Sleeping Venus

Who sleeps here, do you ask? Is she not known,
Your liege-dame Venus, in her sleep of stone?
Waken her not: though she will do no ill,
If waken her you do, no doubt she will
Open her beauteous eyes to band your own.

Epigrammes, I, xxxiv

De l'Abbé, & de son valet

Monsieur l'Abbé, & monsieur son Valet
Sont faictz esgaulx touts deux comme de cire:
L'ung est grand fol, l'aultre ung petit folet:
L'ung veult railler, l'aultre gaudir, & rire:
L'ung boit du bon: l'aultre ne boit du pire:
Mais ung debat au soir entre eulx s'esmeut,
Car maistre Abbé toute la nuict ne veult
Estre sans vin, que sans secours ne meure:
Et son valet jamais dormir ne peult
Tandis qu'au pot une goute en demeure.

Of the Abbé and His Varlet

The abbé and his man are of one kind—
One pod, two peas—each in his wine immersed:
One big, one little, but both much inclined
To madcap revels in the name of thirst;
One drinks the best, the other spurns the worst.
But come the evening they will disagree:
Monsieur *l'abbé* cannot, the night long, be
Without the succor of his alcohol;
And monsieur varlet cannot sleep if he
Has not drunk down the flagon, dregs and all.

Epigrammes, I, XLVI

De frere Thibault

Frere Thibault sejourné, gros, & gras,
Tiroit de nuict une garse en chemise
Par le treillys de sa chambre: où le bras
Elle passa, puis la teste y a mise,
Puis tout le sein: mais elle fut bien prise,
Car son fessier y passer ne sceut onc:
Par la morbieu (ce dict le Moyne adonc)
Il ne me chault de bras, tetin, ne teste:
Passez le cul, ou vous retirez donc:
Je ne sçauroys (sans luy) vous faire feste.

Of Brother Thibault

Brother Thibault—monk lazy, big, and fat—
Was tugging through the lattice of his cell,
One night, a whore, in but a shift; whereat,
Though head, and arms, and breasts came through quite well,
Soon did she stand stuck fast; for, truth to tell,
Her buttocks would not pass, hard though she tried.
"Good God above!" the randy cleric cried,
"Head, arms, and tits indeed! Be quick about it:
Pass me your ass, or get the rest outside!
What would you have me do with you without it!"

Epigrammes, I, XLVII

A ung quidem

Veulx tu sçavoir, à quelle fin
Je t'ay mys hors des œuvres miennes?
Je l'ay faict tout expres, affin
Que tu me mectes hors des tiennes.

To a Certain Person

Why is it, in the verse I write,
That never do I mention you?
It is so that, myself, I might
From yours be ever absent too.

Epigrammes, I, L

Du beau Tetin*

Tetin refect, plus blanc, qu'ung œuf,
Tetin de satin blanc tout neuf,
Tetin, qui fays honte à la Rose,
Tetin plus beau, que nulle chose,
Tetin dur, non pas tetin voyre,
Mais petite boule d'Ivoyre,
Au milieu duquel est assise
Une Fraize, ou une Cerise,
Que nul ne voit, ne touche aussi,
Mais je gage, qu'il est ainsi:
Tetin doncq au petit bout rouge,
Tetin, qui jamais ne se bouge,
Soit pour venir, soit pour aller,
Soit pour courir, soit pour baller:
Tetin gauche, Tetin mignon,
Tousjours loing de son compaignon,
Tetin, qui porte tesmoignage
Du demeurant du personnage,
Quand on te voit, il vient à maints
Une envie dedans les mains
De te taster, de te tenir:
Mais il se fault bien contenir
D'en approcher, bon gré ma vie,
Car il viendroit une autre envie.

O Tetin ne grand, ne petit,
Tetin meur, Tetin d'appetit,
Tetin, qui nuict, & jour criez,

*Uncharacteristically long for an epigram, this piece, written in 1535 and published the following year, quickly achieved immense popularity throughout France, initiating the genre of the *blason,* in which, for a decade, poets would vie with one another in the description of various parts of the female anatomy. (See, inter alia, C. A. Mayer, *Les Epigrammes* [London:

Of the Fair Breast

Breast, whiter than an egg, and quite
As smooth as satin, fresh and white;
Breast that would shame the rose; plump Breast,
Of all things known, the loveliest;
Firm Breast; indeed, not Breast at all;
Rather, a small, round ivory ball,
And in the middle, a cherry placed,
Or berry, and with such beauty graced
That, though I neither touch nor see
It bare, I vow such must it be.
Breast red-tipped; Breast taut, and that never
Waggles about, whithersoever,
Coming or going, running, leaping;
Left Breast—coy, sweet—your distance keeping,
Properly, from your mate, discreet.
Breast that reflects, from top to teat,
The body whole of your possessor!
Ah! Were I but her breast-caresser!
Many's the man that, when he sees you,
Tingles with lust to hold and squeeze you;
But he must rein his appetite,
Never draw near lest soon he might
Burn with a fire quite otherwise!

O Breast of perfect shape and size,
Alluring Breast, who, night and day,
Cry: "Find me a husband, quick, I pray!"

Athlone, 1970], p. 156.) The *blason* is a descriptive poem that praises (or
mocks) one body part detached from the whole: the eyebrow, the teeth, the
cheek, the ear, the hair, and so on. Thanks to Marot's initiative, the genre
reached its high point in the *Blasons anatomiques du corps féminin,* and the
great poets of the age—among them Scève, Mellin de Saint-Gelais, Antoine
Héroët, and several other Pléiade poets—competed with one another to
write examples that were witty and often bizarre. [HG]

Mariez moy tost, mariez,
Tetin, qui t'enfles, & repoulses
Ton gorgerin de deux bons poulses,
A bon droict heureux on dira
Celluy, qui de laict t'emplira,
Faisant d'ung Tetin de pucelle
Tetin de femme entiere, & belle.

Breast swelling full and comely; Breast
Quick to add inches to her chest;
Ah! Right the man who says that he
Is blest who fills you generously
With milk, to turn you, *ma petite,*
From virgin's Breast to Breast complete.

Epigrammes, I, LXXIX

Du laid Tetin*

Tetin, qui n'as rien, que la peau,
Tetin flac, Tetin de drappeau,
Grand' Tetine, longue Tetasse,
Tetin, doy je dire bezasse?
Tetin au grand vilain bout noir,
Comme celluy d'ung entonnoir,
Tetin, qui brimballe à touts coups
Sans estre esbranlé, ne secoux,
Bien se peult vanter, qui te taste,
D'avoir mys la main à la paste:
Tetin grillé, Tetin pendant,
Tetin flestry, Tetin rendant
Vilaine bourbe en lieu de laict,
Le Diable te feit bien si laid:
Tetin pour trippe reputé,
Tetin, ce cuydé je, emprunté,
Ou desrobé en quelcque sorte
De quelque vieille Chievre morte:
Tetin propre pour en Enfer
Nourrir l'enfant de Lucifer:
Tetin boyau long d'une gaule,
Tetasse à jecter sur l'espaule
Pour faire (tout bien compassé)
Ung chapperon du temps passé,
Quand on te voyt, il vient à maints
Une envye dedans les mains
De te prendre avec des gans doubles
Pour en donner cinq, ou six couples
De soufflets sur le nez de celle

*Regarding the success of this *contreblason,* counterpoise to the preceding, and Marot's self-justification for having composed it, see Mayer, *Epigrammes,* p. 158. [NRS]

Of the Ugly Breast

Breast, nothing more than scraggy skin;
Breast with no solid flesh therein;
Sagging and loose, like swaying flag,
Or—dare I say?—a saddlebag!
Black gross-tipped teat, long, ugly (very!),
Funnel-like, that an ordinary
Touch will set wagging in the breeze.
And should, perchance, one choose to seize
Your flaccid form, well may he crow:
"I lend a hand to knead sour dough!"★
Breast dry as dust, breast drooping free;
Breast withered, limp, whence loathsomely
Not milk but muck comes oozing, spewing:
Vile Breast, the very devil's doing.
Breast foul as tripe; Breast I would not
Be much bemused to learn was got
From some old she-goat, lying dead;
Breast wrought in Hell, that might have fed
Lucifer's child; long, swagging sack
Fit to be slung athwart the back,
Over the shoulder, like a cape
Of yesteryear, round neck and nape.
Many's the hand that, when one sees you,
Quakes with disgust, forthwith, to squeeze you—
Well gloved, perforce!—and flail the face
Of her who hides you in disgrace.
Pendulous Breast, gaunt, misbegotten,

★My somewhat free translation attempts to get across the two meanings of the expression *mettre la main à la pâte:* literally, "to knead dough," and figuratively, "to help with a task." [NRS]

Qui te cache soubs son esselle.
Va grand villain Tetin puant,
Tu fourniroys bien en suant
De civettes, & de parfuns
Pour faire cent mille deffunctz.

  Tetin de laydeur despiteuse,
Tetin, dont Nature est honteuse,
Tetin des vilains le plus brave,
Tetin, dont le bout tousjours bave,
Tetin faict de poix, & de glus:
Bren ma plume, n'en parlez plus,
Laissez le là, ventre sainct George,
Vous me feriez rendre ma gorge.

Ah, what a smell, abhorrent, rotten,
Wafts from the sweat that you secrete:
Civets and scents galore, replete
With stench, I warrant, that might choke
A hundred thousand gentlefolk.

   Breast that makes nature blush with shame
To call you Breast; you who defame
The very name of Breast; the first
Among the foulest and the worst;
Breast with your nipple suppurating
Slime—putrid, noxious, nauseating...
By George!—the saint, that is—no more!
Shit, pen, be still! Be silent, or,
If you keep writing so, no doubt
I'll retch and puke my innards out.

Epigrammes, I, LXXX

A Anne★

Anne, ma sœur, sur ces maints Epigrammes
Jecte tes yeulx doulcement regardants:
Et en lisant, si d'amour ne t'enflammes,
A tout le moins ne mesprises les flammes,
Qui pour t'amour luysent icy dedans.

★This epigram introduces some fifty-five pieces supposedly inspired by Marot's love of Anne d'Alençon, *nièce par alliance* of Marguerite de Navarre, and Marot's "sœur." (See also *Epigrammes,* II, xxxviii, for a fuller treatment of the anguish Anne inflicts on him.) [HG]

For Anne

Sweet sister Anne, I pray you cast your glance
Gently upon my Epigrams herein.
If passion burn not hot beneath your skin,
At least scorn not my fires, nor look askance
On flames that, for your love, flare bright within.

Epigrammes, II, 1

De la Royne de Navarre★

Entre aultres dons de grâces immortelles
Ma Dame escript si hault, & doulcement,
Que je m'estonne, en voyant choses telles,
Qu'on n'en reçoit plus d'esbahyssement.

Puis quand je l'oy parler si sagement,
Et que je voy sa plume travailler,
Je tourne bride, & m'esbahy, comment
On est si sot de s'en esmerveiller.

★This encomium to Marguerite de Navarre, sister of François I and icon
of the age, sums up in its pithiness the admiration—and often servile adula-
tion—proffered by the literati and intellectuals of the period. Marguerite
protected Marot when he fled the kingdom in 1534 under accusations of
heresy. The notorious Affair of the Placards triggered the persecution of the

Of the Queen of Navarre

When, midst her other graces, heaven-sent,
Milady, with her gentle grandeur plies
Her pen, I stand in such bewilderment
That my awe any greater awe defies.

But when I hear her speak—sage, worldly wise
The thoughts her pen and tongue so well express—
I turn about, more awed at my surprise,
Bewildered at my blind foolhardiness.

Epigrammes, II, IV

Protestants and evangelical Christians who had posted bills around the king-
dom to denounce the Catholic mass. Marot took refuge in Nérac, in the
kingdom of Navarre, where Marguerite had her court, until he was allowed
to return to France in 1536. François Rabelais was also protected by Mar-
guerite, to whom he dedicated his *Third Book of the Adventures of Pantagruel*
(1546). [HG]

De l'Amour chaste*

Amoureux suis, & Venus estonnée
De mon amour, là où son feu deffault:
Car ma Dame est à l'honneur tant donnée,
Tant est bien chaste, & conditionnée,
Et tant cherchant le bien, qui point ne fault,
Que de l'aymer aultrement, qu'il ne fault,
Seroit ung cas par trop dur, & amer:
Elle est (pourtant) bien belle, & si le vault,
Mais quand je sens son cueur si chaste, & hault,
Je l'ayme tant, que je ne l'ose aymer.

*This poem appeared in 1538 when Neoplatonic love philosophy, following the Florentine philosopher Ficino, was being disseminated in France in Latin and, in the 1540s, in Italian and French through translations of Plato's *Symposium* and Ficino's *Commentary on Plato's Symposium*. Here, Marot repeats the paradox that to love is actually to refrain from expressing love, because discourse and, of course, the embodiment of love rob it of its unique spiritual identification with the Good. [HG]

Of a Chaste Love

In love am I, but with a love so pure,
So passion-free, that Venus, with wide eyes
Looks on, in awe at such a chaste amour;
For honor is milady's signature:
He who would be her beau must realize
That loving her in an unseemly wise
Bespeaks a love unfit, love misbegot.
Comely is she, but, as you may surmise,
When I reflect how pure and chaste the prize,
I love so well that love her I dare not.

Epigrammes, II, VIII

Contre les Jaloux

De ceulx, qui tant de mon bien se tourmentent,
J'ay d'une part grande compassion:
Puis me font rire, en voyant qu'ilz augmentent
Dedans m'amye ung feu d'affection:
Ung feu, lequel par leur invention
Cuydent estaindre. O la paouvre cautelle!
Ilz sont plus loing de leur intention,
Qu'ilz ne vouldroyent que je fusse loing d'elle.

Against the Jealous Ones

Pity I have for those poor fools who eye
My heart's good fortune with a deep dismay.
I laugh to see their envy go awry
As hotter grows my wench's fire each day;
A fire that, with their falsehoods, they essay
To quench. O vile, their jealous strategy!
Far are they from their goal: as far as they
Would, in their treachery, drive her from me.

Epigrammes, II, XIII

A une Amye

Si le loysir tu as avec l'envie
De me reveoir, ô ma joye esperée,
Je te rendray bon compte de ma vie,
Depuis qu'à toy parlay l'aultre serée:
Ce soir fut court, mais c'est chose asseurée
Que tu m'en peulx donner ung par pitié,
Lequel seroit de plus longue durée,
Et sembleroit plus court de la moytié.

To a Wench

If you have but the time and the desire
To see me once again, O heart's delight,
Well shall I count, recount, what deeds transpire★
Since last I spoke with you one recent night.
Too brief that evening; but believe you might
That if, in pity, you grant me one more,
Long will it last—much longer!—though, aright,
It seem but half the night we spent before.

Epigrammes, II, xvii

★The word "compte" in the original has the double meaning of an ac-
count, in the commercial sense, and a story (in modern French, *le conte*).
(Renaissance love poetry often relied on arithmetic to make its point!) I
attempt to transmit something of the duality in my translation. [NRS]

A la bouche de Diane

Bouche de Coral precieux,
Qui à baiser semblez semondre:
Bouche, qui d'ung cueur gracieux
Sçavez tant bien dire, & respondre,
Respondez moy, doibt mon cueur fondre
Devant vous, comme au feu la cyre?
Voulez bien celluy occire,
Qui crainct vous estre desplaisant?
Ha bouche, que tant je desire,
Dictes nenny, en me baisant.

To the Mouth of Diana

O mouth of precious coral hue,
Who seem to beg a kiss; mouth that,
Though gracious-hearted, show that you
Know how to give one tit for tat;
Tell me: must my heart melt thereat,
Before you, as wax in the fire?
Must he who dreads to raise your ire
Perish from fear lest you display it?
Ah! Mouth, object of my desire,
Say "Nay," and kiss me as you say it.

Epigrammes, II, XXIV

A une, qui faisoit la longue

Quand je vous ayme ardantement,
Vostre beaulté toute aultre efface:
Quand je vous ayme froidement
Vostre beaulté fond, comme glace.
Hastez vous de me faire grâce,
Sans trop user de cruaulté,
Car si mon amytié se passe,
A Dieu command vostre beaulté.

To a Lady Too Long Delaying

When I love you with heated passion
Your beauty has no peer. But oh!
When I love you in cooler fashion
Your beauty melts like ice. And so
Make haste and grace me: be not slow,
Lest, dawdling—once my love has flown—
Cruel wench, delighting in my woe,
Your beauty will please God alone.

Epigrammes, II, xxvi

A une Dame eagée, & prudente

Ne pensez point, que ne soyez aymable:
Vostre eage est tant de grâces guerdonné,
Qu'à touts les coups ung Printemps estimable
Pour vostre Yver seroit abandonné:
Je ne suis point Paris Juge estonné
Qui faveur feit à beaulté qui s'efface:
Par moy le pris à Pallas est donné,
De qui on voit l'ymage en vostre face.

To a Lady Agèd and Wise

Think not, madame, that love has fled from you:
Grace crowns your age; and spring, though fair its guise,
Will ever be dispatched and bade adieu
In favor of your winter, chill but wise.
No Paris am I, judge whose awestruck eyes
Preferred mere beauty though it leaves no trace;
For me, Pallas Athena wins the prize,
Whose image one sees clearly on your face.★

Epigrammes, II, xxxvii

★The unnamed object of Marot's apostrophe would, one imagines, take
cold comfort in the consolation that, obviously no Helen of Troy worthy of
the lust of a Paris, she was at least favored by the goddess of wisdom. [NRS]

A Anne

Anne ma Sœur,★ d'où me vient le songer,
Qui toute nuict par devers vous me maine?
Quel nouvel Hoste est venu se loger
Dedans mon cueur, & tousjours s'y pourmaine?
Certes je croy (& ma foy n'est point vaine)
Que c'est ung dieu: me vient il consoller?
Ha, c'est Amour, je le sens bien voller.
Anne, ma Sœur, vous l'avez faict mon Hoste,
Et le sera (me deust il affoller)
Si celle là, qui l'y mist, ne l'en oste.

★Gérard Defaux suggests that "Anne, ma Sœur" echoes Virgil's phrase "Anna Soror" (*Aeneid* 4.9–12), in which Dido, the spurned lover of Aeneas, confides her passion for the Trojan warrior to her sister, Anne. (See Defaux 2:1063.) This is an example of how Marot translated Virgil and adapted him to his own purpose. [HG]

To Anne

Sweet Anne, whence comes this dream that, ceaselessly,
Draws me to you each night? Who is this guest
Unbidden, newly come to lodge with me
Within my heart, prowl, rob me of my rest?
Some god, perhaps, to soothe my harried breast—
Unless I err—and keep me company?
Ah! Love it is, the wingèd Cupid he.
Sweet Anne, you placed him there, there must he stay,
Though he deprive me of my sanity,
If she who brought him bears him not away.

Epigrammes, II, xxxviii

Du Baiser*

Ce franc Baiser, ce Bayser amyable,
Tant bien donné, tant bien receu aussi,
Qu'il estoit doulx! O beaulté admirable!
Baisez moy doncq cent foys le jour ainsi,
Me recevant dessoubs vostre mercy
Pour tout jamais: ou vous pourrez bien dire,
Qu'en me donnant ung Baiser adoulcy,
M'aurez donné perpetuel martyre.

*See the Dutch-born Neo-Latin poet Jean Second (Johannes Secundus, 1511–1536), whose collection of poems *Basia* (1539, 1541) became the model for kiss poems by Marot, Ronsard, and many others in sixteenth-century France. [HG]

Of the Kiss

That honest kiss, that kiss so pure, discreet,
Bestowed so lovingly, received no less,
How sweet it was! Milady, I entreat
Your grace to kiss me with yet more largesse,
A hundred times a day, O loveliness,
Eternal captor mine, lest I become—
With that one kiss—condemned to dire duress
And to an everlasting martyrdom.

Epigrammes, II, LII

Des Cerfz en rut, & des Amoureux

Les cerfz en rut pour les Bisches se battent,
Les Amoureux pour les Dames combattent,
Ung mesme effect engendre leurs discords:
Les Cerfz en rut d'amour brament, & crient,
Les Amoureux gemissent, pleurent, prient,
Eulx, & les cerfz feroyent de beaulx accords:
Amants sont Cerfz à deux pieds soubs ung corps,
Ceulx cy à quatre: & pour venir aux testes,
Il ne s'en fault, que ramures, & cors,
Que vous Amants ne soyez aussi bestes.

Of Stags in Rut and Lovers

    Young stags in rut do battle for their does,
And, for their damsels, likewise do our beaus;
Bringing to life the same disharmony,
One cause it is that fuels their enmity.
Young stags in rut bellow, and wail, and bray;
Our beaus whine, weep their love, beseech, and pray:
The difference? Lovers have two feet: indeed,
Our stags have four; as for their heads, I guess
Antlers and horns are all you lovers need
To match them in their beastly foolishness.

Epigrammes, II, LVIII

De sa Dame, & de soymesme

Des que m'Amye est ung jour sans me veoir,
Elle me dict, que j'en ay tardé quatre:
Tardant deux jours, elle dict ne m'avoir
Veu de quatorze, & n'en veult rien rabatre:
Mais pour l'ardeur de mon Amour abatre,
De ne la veoir j'ay raison apparente.
Voyez, Amants, nostre Amour differente:
Languir la fays, quand suis loing de ses yeulx:
Mourir me faict, quand je la voy presente.
Jugez lequel vous semble aymer le mieulx.

Of His Lady and Himself

If for one day milady sees me not,
She says for four I tarry; and if two,
Says she fourteen, nor will she budge a jot.
No matter: true it is I should eschew
Her quite, if I my passion would subdue,
And from her sight remain afar. But then,
How different are we lovers twain; for when
She pines and sees me not, she sighs, heartsore;
But I, each time I see her, die again:
Which of the two, I ask you, loves the more?

Epigrammes, II, XL

D'un gros Prieur

Un gros Prieur son petit fils baisoit,
Et mignardoit au matin en sa couche,
Tandis rostir sa Perdrix on faisoit:
Se leve, crache, esmeutit, & se mouche:
La Perdrix vire: Au sel de broque en bouche
La devora, bien sçavoit la science:
Puis quand il eut prins sur sa conscience
Broc de vin blanc, du meilleur qu'on eslise:
Mon Dieu, dit il, donne moy patience,
Qu'on a de maulx, pour servir saincte Église!

Of a Fat Prior

A prior, fat, one morning, playfully
Kisses his cradled baby son, with "ohs"
And "ahs"; watches his partridge roast; then he
Gets to his feet, spits, shits, and blows his nose.
The partridge turns; he salts it as it goes
Round on the skewer; wolfs it down: well-versed
Was he in kitchen science; then, a-thirst,
Calming his conscience with a jug of wine—
Fine, white—"Damn! Give me patience, God!" he cursed.
"What pains we go to for our Church divine!"

Epigrammes, III, xxxvii

Huictain*

Plus ne suis ce que j'ay esté,
Et ne le sçaurois jamais estre.
Mon beau printemps, & mon esté,
Ont faict le sault par la fenestre.
Amour, tu as esté mon maistre,
Je t'ay servy sur tous les Dieux.
O, si je povois deux fois naistre,
Comment je te serviroys mieulx!

*Other editors give this brief bit of nostalgia a less clinically objective title: "De Soy-mesme" ("Of Himself"). [NRS]

Octave

What once I was I am no more,
And nevermore shall find it;
Sweet spring went bounding through the door
With summer close behind it.★
I labored, Love, in your employ,
No god had keener servant.
Ah! could I second birth enjoy,
I should be yet more fervent!

Epigrammes, III, LIII

★For readers interested in the translation process and the ever-present
problems of choice that it poses, I offer an alternative version of these lines,
more faithful to the letter of the text: "Sweet spring leapt through the
window, for / Summer chased close behind it." Preferring each for different
reasons, I flipped a coin. [NRS]

A ung jeune Escolier docte, griefvement malade

Charles, mon fils, prenez courage,
Le beau temps vient apres l'orage,
Apres maladie santé.
Dieu a trop bien en vous planté
Pour perdre ainsi son labourage.

To a Learned Young Scholar, Grievously Ill

Charles, son, take heart; do not bemoan
Your state: sun shines when storm has flown;
When illness leaves health blooms anew.
God planted too much good in you
To waste the seeds his hand has sown.

Epigrammes, III, LIX

D'un Moyne & d'une vieille*

Le Moyne un jour jouant sus la riviere
Trouva la vieille en lavant ses drapeaux,
Qui luy monstra de sa cuisse heronniere
Un feu ardant où joignoient les deux peaux.
Le Moyne eut cueur, leve ses oripeaux:
Il prend son chose, & puis, s'aprochant d'elle,
Vieille, dist il, allumez ma chandelle!†
La vieille lors, luy voulant donner bon,
Tourne son cul, & respond par cautelle:
Aprochez vous, & souflez au charbon.

---

*For a possible, even probable, Latin source of this bawdy scenario, in the *Facetiarum Libri Tres* of Heinrich Bebel (1542), see Defaux 2:1130. [HG]

†The word *chandelle* for penis is found routinely in medieval fabliaux and Renaissance narratives. For example, see Philippe de Vigneulles, *Les Cent Nouvelles nouvelles* (ca. 1515): "Voici maître curé qui vient pour allumer sa chandelle, ou pour mieux dire l'éteindre" (Here comes master parson to light his candle or, better, to copulate [literally, "to blow it out"]). [HG]

Of a Monk and a Crone

A monk, along a river, idly playing,
Found a crone in her tattered fripperies
Washing her rags, her scrawny thighs betraying
Fire in the flesh, above and 'twixt the knees.
Boldly our monk lifts high his trappings, frees
That thing of his, approaches. "Crone," says he,
"Come light my candle!" Brash her repartee.
Down she bows, low, her rump thrusts in the air,
And, turning it to face him, says: "Let's see
If you can blow the coals to life, *mon frère!*"

Epigrammes, III, LXXIV

Du tetin de Cataut

    Celuy qui dit bon ton tetin
N'est mensonger, mais veritable:
Car je t'asseure, ma Catin,
Qu'il m'est tresbon, & agreable.
Il est tel, & si profitable
Que si du nez hurtoit quelqu'un,
Contre iceluy (sans nulle fable)
Il ne se feroit mal aucun.

Of Cataut's Breast

Cataut, dear whore,★ who would admire
Your beauteous breast need tell no lies;
Rather, he speaks the truth entire:
I find it of the best, and prize
Its fullness, comely shape, and size;
And should one's nose upon it hit,
I can assure you, in no wise
Would his nose be the worse for it.†

Epigrammes, III, LXXVIII

★Cataut, a diminutive of Catherine, fortunately fallen into disuse, implied in Marot's time the same easy virtue (or absence of same) as the noun *catin,* in use then and still met with today, though rather dated. [NRS]

†A note in Defaux 2:1132 explains the reference to the nose as an allusion to a passage in chapter 40 of *Gargantua,* in which Rabelais claims that hard-breasted wet nurses give babies snub noses. [NRS]

D'un Cordelier

Un Cordelier d'une assez bonne mise
Avoit gaigné à je ne sçay quel jeu
Chausses, pourpoint, & la belle chemise.
En cest estat son hostesse l'a veu,
Qui luy a dit: vous rompez vostre veu.
Non, non, respond ce gracieux records,
Je l'ay gaigné au travail de mon corps,
Chausses, chemise, & pourpoint pourfilé.
Puis dist (tirant son grand tribard dehors):
Ce beau fuzeau a tout fait & filé.

Of a Franciscan

A monk Franciscan—pleasant was his mien—
Gaming, had won (I know not where nor how)
Fine waistcoat, hose, and shift; whence he was seen
By one who ofttimes gave him alms. "Well now,"
Said she, "it seems you much disdain your vow!"
"Nay!" disaccords our gentle Cordelier,★
"Much has my body toiled to make what here
I wear: hose, waistcoat, shift, second to none!"
Whereat he, rod in hand, says in her ear:
"See this fine spindle wherewith I have spun!"

Epigrammes, III, LXXX

★My translation attempts to produce something akin to Marot's obvious
wordplay on "records" (witness) and "Cordelier." [NRS]

**A une Dame de Piemont, qui refusa six escuz de Marot
pour coucher avec elle & en vouloit avoir dix**

Ma dame, je vous remercie
De m'avoir esté si rebourse.
Pensez vous que je m'en soucye,
Ne que tant soit peu m'en courrousse?
Nanny, non. Et pourquoy? & pour-ce
Que six escuz sauvez m'avez,
Qui sont aussi bien en ma bourse,★
Que dans le trou que vous sçavez.

★Given the context, it is tempting to suppose that Marot was in some way
intending, at least indirectly, a play on the word *bourse,* which, in addition to
its meaning of purse, has, since the twelfth century, also meant scrotum.
[NRS]

**For a Lady from the Piedmont, Who Refused to Let Marot
Sleep with Her for Six Crowns and Who Asked for Ten**

    Thank you, Madame, most kindly for
Denying me your company.
Think you I care the slightest, or
That it annoys or angers me?
Nay, not a whit! Why? Well, you see,
I save six crowns; though you abhor 'em,
My purse will house them graciously,
More than that hole where you would store 'em.

Epigrammes, III, LXXXII

D'un escolier, & d'une fillete

Comme un escolier se jouoit
Avec une belle pucelle,
Pour luy plaire, bien fort louoit
Sa grâce, & beauté naturelle,
Les tetons mignards de la belle,
Et son petit cas, qui tant vaut.
Ha monsieur, adoncq' ce dist elle,
Dieu y mette ce qu'il y faut.

Of a Schoolboy and a Damsel

A schoolboy, dallying apace
With damsel fair—his favorite—
To please her, praised her virgin grace,
Her youthful beauty exquisite:
Her bosom full and firm of tit,
Her you-know-what, *petit* indeed.
"Ah yes!" said she, "But let God fit
Within it all that it may need!"

Epigrammes, III, xc

Dizain

Riche ne suis, certes, je le confesse,
Bien né pourtant, & nourry noblement:
Mais je suis leu du peuple & gentillesse
Par tout le monde. Et, dit on, c'est Clement.
Maintz vivront peu, moy eternellement.
Et toy, tu as prez, fontaines & puyz,
Boys, champs, chasteaux, rentes & gros appuyz.
C'est de nous deux la difference & l'estre:
Mais tu ne peulx estre ce que je suis:
Ce que tu es, ung chascun le peult estre.

"Rich am I not, most surely, I confess"★

Rich am I not, most surely, I confess,
Though well born and well fed; and yet am I
Read by the common folk, and court no less;
They see my verse: "Clément wrote that!" they cry.
Most live but little; I need never die.
You have your fields, and founts, wooded terrains,
Castles, and wells, and wealth, and vast domains.
That is the difference, friend, 'twixt you and me.
You cannot live my life, for all your pains;
But what you are, sire, anyone can be.

Epigrammes, IV, x†

★There being no word in English for the French *dizain* (ten-line verse), I
call on the first line to serve as this epigram's English title, rather than invent
one (for example, "Of Himself and an Ignorant Rich Man"), as some editors
have done. [NRS]

†All the epigrams in Book IV, in the Defaux edition, are adaptations of the
Latin satirist Martial, originally published posthumously. For a discussion of
the original volume from which most of them are taken (*Epigrammes de
Clement Marot, faictz à l'imitation de Martial, etc.* [Poitiers: Les Frères Marnef,
1547]), as well as for the Latin text of each, see Defaux 2:1142–1159. [NRS]

De Cathin et Jane

Jadis, Cathin,★ tu estoys l'oultrepasse:
Jane à present toutes les aultres passe.
Et pour donner l'arrest d'entre vous deux,
Elle sera ce de quoy tu te deulz:
Tu ne seras jamais de sa valuë.
Que faict le temps? Il fait que je la veulx,
Et que je t'ay aultrefoys bien vouluë.

★Cat(h)in, like Cat(h)aut, was a pejorative nickname for Catherine. (See p. 139, note.) [NRS]

Of Cathin and Jeanne

You, Cathin, once upon a time, were quite
The *ne plus ultra,* source of all delight.
Now Jeanne surpasses every belle, and you,
Alas, are much the lesser of the two.
Never again will you be what you were,
Or what she is; time does what it must do:
Once I desired you, now I lust for her.

Epigrammes, IV, XVIII

De Pauline

    Pauline est riche, et me veult bien
Pour mary: Je n'en feray rien,
Car tant vieille est que j'en ay honte.
S'elle estoit plus vieille du tiers,
Je la prendrois plus voulentiers:
Car depesche en seroit plus prompte.

Of Pauline

Pauline is rich and fain would choose
Me for her husband: I refuse;
So old is she, I scorn and scoff.
If older by a third she were,
Then happily would I concur,
For soon would she be shuffling off.

Epigrammes, IV, XXII

De la Formis enclose en de l'Ambre

Dessoubz l'Arbre où l'Ambre degoute
La petite Formis alla:
Sur elle en tumba une goutte,
Qui tout à coup se congela:
Dont la Formis demoura là,
Au milieu de l'Ambre enfermée.
Ainsi la beste deprisée,
Et peu prisée quand elle vivoit,
Est à sa mort fort estimée,
Quand si beau sepulchre on luy voit.

Of the Ant Enclosed in Amber

An ant, beneath a tree a-dripping
With amber sap, her course was plying:
A drop fell as she went a-tripping,
Laying her low; soon she lay dying
In sap entrapped, solidifying,
In amber grave immortalized.
Thus is it that, in life despised,
And to disdain unkindly doomed,
The beast, in death, is highly prized
When in rich sepulcher entombed.

Epigrammes, IV, xxiv

Du Curé. Imitation★

   Au curé, ainsi comme il dit,
Plaisent toutes belles femelles,
Et ont envers luy grand credit
Tant Bourgeoyses, que Damoyselles.
Si luy plaisent les femmes belles
Autant qu'il dit, je n'en sçay rien:
Mais une chose sçay je bien:
Qu'il ne plaist à pas une d'elles.

★I suspect that Marot's unusual assurance that this is merely an imitation as opposed, perhaps, to a real translation—if, indeed, it was his own addition and not an editor's—results from the fact that the model for this epigram (Martial, "In Faustum" 2.65) is a pithy elegiac couplet: "Nescio tam multis quid scribas, Fauste, puellis, / Hoc scio, quod scribit nulla puella tibi." [NRS]

Of the Priest (An Imitation)

The *curé* has—or so he claims—
For females fair a tender feeling,
And treats them all—damsels, beldames—
With great affection in his dealing.
Now, if that taste he is revealing—
Love of the gentle sex—be so,
I cannot say; but this I know:
Not one of them finds him appealing.

Epigrammes, IV, xxxii

Baiser volé★

Vous vous plaingnez de mon audace,
Qui ay prins de vous ung baiser
Sans en requerir vostre grace.
Venez vers moy vous appaiser:
Je ne vous iray plus baiser
Sans vostre congé; veu qu'ainsi
Il vous deult de ce baiser cy,
Lequel, si bien l'ay osé prendre,
N'est pas perdu: je suis icy
En bon vouloir de le vous rendre.

★Though it is found in other collections of Marot's *Epigrammes,* this one
does not occur in the Defaux edition, which would lead me to suspect its
authenticity. I include it nonetheless, hoping that, with its typical *élégant
badinage,* it may eventually prove to be of his making. [NRS]

Stolen Kiss

I stole a kiss from you without
Your leave; and thus do you complain
That I am an audacious lout.
Come here, and let me ease your pain:
I will not kiss you yet again
Save you consent; for with that kiss
I grieved you, handled you amiss,
That kiss I filched without ado,
And kept; but I will tell you this:
Fain would I give it back to you.

JOACHIM DU BELLAY.
Né en 1524. Mort en 1560.

C. J. Boucher del et inv. ex Bibliotheca Regia

Joachim Du Bellay

(1522? – 1560)

Recueil de poésie

Vers lyriques

L'Olive

XIII Sonnetz de l'honneste amour

Les Antiquitez de Rome

Les Regrets

Divers Jeux rustiques

Les Amours

Sonnets divers

Note: The original Du Bellay texts are reproduced from four volumes of the eight-volume *Œuvres poétiques,* critical edition prepared by Henri Chamard for the Société des Textes Français Modernes: 1 (Paris, 1908; augmented edition by Yvonne Bellenger [Paris: Nizet, 1982]); 2 (Paris, n.d.; new edition, Paris: Bordat, 1993); 3 (Paris, 1912; new edition, Paris: Nizet, 1983); and 5 (Paris, 1923; new edition, Paris: Nizet, 1987), hereinafter cited as Chamard. [NRS]

RECUEIL DE POÉSIE

A sa lyre

Va donques maintenant, ma Lyre,
Ma Princesse te veult ouir.
Il fault sa table docte elire:
Là, quelque amy voudra bien lire
Tes chansons, pour la resjouir.

Ta voix encores basse & tendre
Apren à hausser des ici,
Et fay tes chordes si bien tendre,
Que mon grand Roy te puisse entendre,
Et sa royale epouze aussi.

Il ne fault que l'envieux die
Que trop hault tu as entrepris:
Ce qui te fait ainsi hardie,
C'est que les choses qu'on dedie
Au temple, sont de plus grand pris.

To His Lyre

Go now, O Lyre of mine! Go fly!
My Princess fain would hear your voice.
Unto her learned guests draw nigh:
There a friend, doubtless, by and by,
Will, with your songs, her heart rejoice.★

Sing higher than is your wont: too low
And tender is your tone, I fear.
Let your chords go a-soaring, so
That, when round and about they go,
My great King and his Queen may hear.

Let not the envious soul complain
That you have aimed too high, my Lyre:
Bold you may be, but I maintain,
Poems for those of high demesne
Capture the prize and rise the higher.

Recueil de poésie

★The princess in question is Marguerite de France, sister of Henri II, to whom the entire collection of the twenty-one poems of the *Recueil de poésie*, first published in 1549, was dedicated, and who is also the subject of two of its odes. This introductory poem to the collection expresses in verse the prose sentiments of Du Bellay's flattering preface. As for the friend alluded to, no doubt another of Marguerite's admirers, Henri Chamard suggests in his critical edition (*Œuvres poétiques* 3:60) that it is Jacques Bouju. A native of Du Bellay's Anjou, Bouju (1515–1577) wrote poetry in Latin and French, none of which seems to have been published, and is mentioned often in the works of Du Bellay and Ronsard. [NRS]

VERS LYRIQUES

Du premier jour de l'an
AU SEIGNEUR BERTRAN BERGIER★

Voicy le Pere au double front,
Le bon Janus, qui renouvelle
Le cours de l'an, qui en un rond
Ameine la saison nouvelle.
   Renouvelons aussi
   Toute vieille pensée,
   Et tuons le soucy
   De fortune insensée.

Sus doncq', que tardons-nous encore?
Avant que vieillars devenir,
Chassons le soing, qui nous devore
Trop curieux de l'advenir.
   Ce qui viendra demain
   Ja pensif ne te tienne:
   Les Dieux ont en leur main
   Ta fortune & la mienne.

★Bertrand Bergier de Montembeuf, of Poitiers, whom Du Bellay honored with two other dedications, was himself a poet, admired by Ronsard as well as by their Pléiade colleague, poet Antoine de Baïf. (See Chamard 3:26.) [NRS]

Of the First Day of the Year
TO SEIGNEUR BERTRAN BERGIER

Father with double brow, behold!
Good Janus, who, in endless ring,
Joining the new unto the old,
Another year is fashioning.
    And so let us, in turn,
    Refashion thoughts outworn,
    And kill all vain concern
    For morrows yet unborn.

Come now, why do we still delay?
Away with all-consuming woe!
Forget tomorrow, live today:
We shall not any younger grow.
    The future soon appears—
    The Gods hold all the strings—
    Nor can your brooding fears
    Avert the fate it brings.

Tu voy de nege tous couvers
Les sommetz de la forest nue,
Qui quasi envoye à l'envers
Le faiz de sa teste chenue.★
    La froide bize ferme
    Le gosier des oyzeaux,
    Et les poissons enferme
    Soubz le cristal des eaux.

Veux-tu attendre les frimaz
De l'hyver, qui deja s'appreste,
Pour faire de nege un amaz
Sur ton menton & sur ta teste?
    Que tes membres transiz
    Privez de leur verdeur,
    Et les nerfz endurciz
    Tremblent tous de froideur?

Quand la saison amolira
Tes braz autresfois durs & roydes,
Adoncq' malgré toy perira
Le feu de tes moüelles froydes,
    Que toute herbe ou etuve,
    Tout genial repas,
    Mais tout l'Aethne & Vesuve
    Ne rechaufferoint pas.

★The comparison between snow-capped trees and the "teste chenue" (hoary head) of an old man is a well-worn figure in French medieval and Renaissance verse. Rhetorically, this is the *similitudo* of the Ancients, a particularly apt device to express the comparative perspective of poets whose writing, as in that of the Pléiade poets, was accomplished in rapport with classical writers and genres. [HG]

Behold the forest peaks bedecked
With snow that, lo! cloaks their undress,
Each drooping treetop, once erect,
Bent low in hoary helplessness.
    The north wind's icy breath
    Shuts tight the songbird's throat,
    And tombs the fish beneath
    The water's crystal coat.

What? will you idly wait until
The snows that winter, even now
Prepares, are scattered deep and chill
Over your aging chin and brow;
    Until no trace is left
    Of bygone salad day,
    And limbs, nerves, life-bereft,
    Tremble their hours away?

For when time weakens you of limb
That once was strong, and straight, and stout,
Then will your marrow-fire grow dim
In spite of you, and flicker out;
    No physic, no receipt,
    No thermal regimen,
    Nor all Vesuvius' heat
    Will kindle it again.

Mon filz, c'est assez combatu,
(Disoit la mere au fort Gregeois,)
Pourquoy ne te rejouys-tu
Avecq' ces filles quelques fois?
　　Les vins, l'amour consolent
　　Le triste cœur de l'homme:
　　Les ans legiers s'en volent,
　　Et la mort nous assomme.

Je te souhaite pour t'ebatre
Durant ceste morte saison,
Un plaisir, voyre trois ou quatre,
Que donne l'amye maison:
　　Bon vin en ton celier,
　　Beau feu, nuyt sans soucy,
　　Un amy familier,
　　Et belle amye aussi,

Qui de son luc, qui de sa voix
Endorme souvent tes ennuiz,
Qui de son babil quelquesfois
Te face moins durer les nuitz,
　　Au lict follastre autant
　　Que ces chevres lascives,
　　Lors qu'elles vont broutant
　　Sur les herbeuses rives.

"You have fought long enough, my son,"
Mighty Achilles' mother said;
"Now let this deadly sport be done
And frolic with the maids instead."
    In wine and love the heart
    Finds solace for its pains;
    Swift-winged, the years depart,
    And death alone remains.

In these, the long year's slumber-days,
May you find pleasures, two by two,
To pass the hours in all the ways
A friendly hearth can offer you:
    Bright fire, night warm with cheer,
    Good wine to drink your fill,
    True friend forever near,
    And woman nearer still,

Who, with her lute or with her lay,
Will soothe and temper your distress,
Or while the lingering hours away
With prattle glib and meaningless;
    And in your bed disporting,
    Be all the playful lass,
    Like lustful goat cavorting
    When grazing on the grass.

                Vers lyriques, Ode VI

L'OLIVE

Ce que je sen', la langue ne refuse
Vous decouvrir, quand suis de vous absent,
Mais tout soudain que pres de moy vous sent,
Elle devient & muette & confuse.

Ainsi, l'espoir me promect & m'abuse:
Moins pres je suis, quand plus je suis present:
Ce qui me nuist, c'est ce qui m'est plaisent:
Je quier' cela, que trouver je recuse.

Joyeux la nuit, le jour triste je suis:
J'ay en dormant ce qu'en veillant poursuis:
Mon bien est faulx, mon mal est veritable.

D'une me plain', & deffault n'est en elle:
Fay' doncq', Amour, pour m'estre charitable,
Breve ma vie ou ma nuit eternelle.

My tongue, madame, would eagerly express
My thoughts to you when you bide far away,
But when I feel you close, naught can I say:
Suddenly it falls mute and powerless.

Thus hope both calms and kindles my distress;
Nearer I draw, yet farther seem to stay:
My pleasure is my woe, ah, welladay!
What most I crave, the least dare I possess.

Joyous by night and sad by day am I:
Sleep brings me what my waking hours deny;
The good I feel is false, the ill is true.

Woman I blame, yet faultless is she, quite;
Thus, Love, to ease my pain, I pray that you
Cut short my days, or grant me endless night.

L'Olive, XXVIII⋆

⋆*L'Olive* is the first *canzoniere* in French composed of sonnets. Inspired by
Petrarch, it shows the poet enveloped in paradox, a Petrarchan conceit that
figures the tension of contrary feelings in love. [HG]

O prison doulce, où captif je demeure
Non par dedaing, force ou inimitié,
Mais par les yeulx de ma doulce moitié,
Qui m'y tiendra jusq'à tant que je meure.

O l'an heureux, le mois, le jour & l'heure,
Que mon cœur fut avecq' elle allié!
O l'heureux nœu, par qui j'y fu' lié,
Bien que souvent je plain', souspire & pleure!*

Tous prisonniers, vous etes en soucy,
Craignant la loy & le juge severe:
Moy plus heureux, je ne suis pas ainsi.

Mile doulx motz, doulcement exprimez,
Mil' doulx baisers, doulcement imprimez,
Sont les tormens où ma foy persevere.

*According to Aris and Joukovsky, editors of *Œuvres poétiques* (Paris: Classiques Garnier, 1993), 1:291, the source of this poem's second quatrain is Petrarch's sonnet 61, "Benedetto sia 'l giorno e 'l mese e l'anno." The conceits in this sonnet, such as sweet prison, prisoner, bondage, and eyes, confirm the influence of the *Rime* on Du Bellay's love poems. [HG]

Sweet prison mine, where I in bondage bide,
Held not by force, nor scorn, nor enmity,
But by the eyes of my sweet mistress; she
Whose thrall will last till I, at last, have died.

Happy the year, the month, when first I plied
My love! Happy the day, the hour, when we
Joined heart to heart in joyous harmony,
Though often have I wept, and wailed, and sighed.

O prisoners who, in durance dolorous,
Dread law and judges harsh who brandish it,
Happier I, whom naught discomfits thus;

Sweet blandishments, a thousand, sweetly offered;
Sweet kisses, too, a thousand, sweetly proffered:
These, my faith's torments, endless, infinite.

L'Olive, XXXIII

L'unic oiseau (miracle emerveillable)
Par feu se tue, ennuyé de sa vie:
Puis quand son ame est par flammes ravie,
Des cendres naist un autre à luy semblable.

Et moy qui suis l'unique miserable,
Faché de vivre, une flamme ay suyvie,
Dont conviendra bien tost que je devie,
Si par pitié ne m'etes secourable.

O grand' doulceur! ô bonté souveraine!
Si tu ne veulx dure & inhumaine estre
Soubz ceste face angelique & seraine,

Puis qu'ay pour toy du Phenix le semblant,
Fay qu'en tous poinctz je luy soy' resemblant,
Tu me feras de moymesme renaistre.

Unique, the fabled bird—O wonder rare!—
Surfeited with its life, seeks death by fire;
Then, as its soul is laid waste on the pyre,
Its double, ash-born, rises in the air.

I too, unique in misery and care,
Sated with life no less, in anguish dire,
Soon must needs quit the flame of my desire
If you not pity me, ease my despair.

O peerless grace! O goodness unforeseen!
Lest you would ruthless be, and inhumane,
For all that tranquil and angelic mien,

Since I appear a Phoenix in your eyes,
Let me resemble it in every wise
And, from my ashes born, arise again.

L'Olive, XXXVI

O foible esprit, chargé de tant de peines,
Que ne veulx-tu soubz la terre descendre?
O cœur ardent, que n'es-tu mis en cendre?
O tristes yeulx, que n'estes-vous fonteines?

O bien douteux! ô peines trop certaines!
O doulx sçavoir, trop amer à comprendre!
O Dieu qui fais que tant j'ose entreprendre,
Pourquoy rends-tu mes entreprises vaines?

O jeune archer, archer qui n'as point d'yeulx,
Pourquoy si droict as-tu pris ta visée?
O vif flambeau, qui embrases les Dieux,

Pourquoy as-tu ma froideur attisée?
O face d'ange! ô cœur de pierre dure!
Regarde au moins le torment que j'endure.★

★The rhymed couplet (*rime plate*) in final position is only one way that the
French Renaissance sonnet was configured in its final *sixain* (six-line stanza),
typographically set off in two three-line units, or tercets. For example, the
so-called Italian sonnet (*abba abba ccd eed*) placed a rhymed couplet in lines
nine and ten, creating a third quatrain of the last four lines. The so-called
French sonnet disposed its tercets as follows: *ccd ede.* [HG]

O spirit, weak, weighed down with woes therein,
Why will you not seek earth's repose, entombed?
O burning heart, why lie you not consumed?
O sad eyes, might you not two streams have been?

O fleeting wealth! O all too sure chagrin!
O science sweet, to bitter darkness doomed!
O God, who cause my every deed, new-bloomed,
To come to grief, scarcely though I begin!

O archer, you, young archer dim of eye,
Why have you shot me with such deadly aim?
O torch, who fire the very Gods on high,

Why have you stirred my embers back to flame?
O angel's face! O stone heart, hard and numb!
At least look on my pain, my martyrdom.

L'Olive, LV

Pour mettre en vous sa plus grande beauté,
Le ciel ouvrit ses plus riches thesors:
Amour choisit de ses traictz les plus fors,
Pour me tirer sa plus grand' cruauté.

Les astres n'ont de luire liberté,
Quand le Soleil ses rayons met dehors:
Ou apparoist votre celeste corps,
La beauté mesme y perdroit sa clerté.

Si le torment de mes affections
Croist à l'egal de voz perfections,
Et si en vous plus qu'en moy je demeure,

Pourquoy n'as-tu, ô fiere destinée!
Rompu le fil de ma vie obstinée?
Je ne croy point que de douleur on meure.

Heaven bestowed its rich munificence
Upon you, when your beauty it designed:
Love chose the strongest arrows he could find
To shoot me with his blind malevolence.

When Sun darts forth his rays, the stars commence
To fade, no longer free to gleam; resigned,
Beauty herself must stand, dull and outshined,   *personifying?*
When your celestial body ventures hence.

If thus the torment of my love's distress
Grows all the more, as grows your flawlessness,
If you, more than myself, my soul contain—

O haughty fate!—why have you not, pride-rife,
Broken the thread of my obdurate life?
Alas, I fear one dies not of love's pain.

                                    L'Olive, LXVI

Si nostre vie est moins qu'une journée
En l'eternel, si l'an qui faict le tour
Chasse noz jours sans espoir de retour,
Si perissable est toute chose née,

Que songes-tu, mon ame emprisonnée?
Pourquoy te plaist l'obscur de nostre jour,
Si pour voler en un plus cler sejour,
Tu as au dos l'aele bien empanée?

La, est le bien que tout esprit desire,
La, le repos ou tout le monde aspire,
La, est l'amour, la, le plaisir encore.

La, ô mon ame au plus hault ciel guidée!
Tu y pouras recongnoistre l'Idée
De la beauté, qu'en ce monde j'adore.★

★Du Bellay writes in an age caught up with Neoplatonic love. The notion
that love begins with desire, then raises itself to be one with the idea of
beauty, is derived from Plato, whose *Symposium* had, since its translation into
Latin by Ficino (1484), shaped Continental tastes and philosophies of love, in
particular Neoplatonic love. Ficino's commentary on Plato's *Symposium* was
first rendered into French by a servant of Marguerite de Navarre as *Le
Commentaire de Marsille Ficin, Florentin: sur le banquet d'amour de Platon, faict
françois par Symon Silvius, dit J. de La Haye, valet de chambre de treschréstienne
Princesse Marguerite de France, royne de Navarre* (Poitiers, 1546). Ficino's avatars
included the immensely popular *Dialoghi d'amore* by Leone Ebreo (Lyon,
1551), just two years after the publication of *L'Olive*. [HG]

spiritual ascent

If this, our life, be less than but a day
In the eternal; if each circling year
Bears off our days, never to reappear;
If every creature born must death obey,

sense that time on earth is very-temporary

Why then, my prisoned soul, should you delay?
How can it please you thus to tarry here,
In darkness, when, unto a brighter sphere,
Your well-plumed wings would carry you away?

ascent

There, is the good that man's mind hungers for;
There, the repose he seeks, forevermore;
There, love and joy abound, their bliss bestow.

There, O my soul, as you reach heaven's height,
Beauty ideal will loom within your sight,
That beauty that I worship here below.

subverts poems meaning – does he want to continue to enjoy physical, earthly beauty?

L'Olive, CXIII

XIII SONNETZ DE L'HONNESTE AMOUR

Ce ne sont pas ces beaux cheveux dorez,
Ny ce beau front, qui l'honneur mesme honnore,
Ce ne sont pas les deux archets encore'
De ces beaux yeux de cent yeux adorez:

Ce ne sont pas les deux brins colorez
De ce coral, ces levres que j'adore,
Ce n'est ce teinct emprunté de l'Aurore,
Ny autre object des cœurs enamourez:

Ce ne sont pas ny ces lyz, ny ces rozes,
Ny ces deux rancz de perles si bien closes,
C'est cet esprit, rare present des cieux,

Dont la beauté de cent graces pourvëue
Perce mon ame & mon cœur & mes yeux
Par les rayons de sa poignante vëue.

Neither is it that comely golden hair,
Nor that fair forehead, honor's honored prize;
Neither is it the brows that arch those eyes
That scores of eyes adore in earnest prayer;

Neither is it that bud, that tender pair
Of coral lips, those lips I idolize,
Nor that complexion, drawn from Dawn's pink skies,
Nor all such things the lover's heart finds fair;

Neither is it the lilies nor the roses,
Nor all those perfect pearls her smile discloses:
Rather it is that mind the heavens impart,

Whose beauty graces by the score enhance—
Rare gift!—that pierce my eyes, my soul, my heart,
Darts that transfix me with her every glance.

XIII Sonnetz de l'honneste amour, II

[handwritten annotations: "only in 3rd stanza does he get to what he's saying poem is really about"; "complicates the Neoplatonic ascent w/ this poem"]

Ce Paradis, qui souspire le bâsme,
D'une angelique & saincte gravité
M'ouvre le ryz, mais bien la Deïté,
Ou mon esprit divinement se pâsme.

Ces deux soleilz, deux flambeaux de mon âme,
Pour me rejoindre à la Divinité,
Perçent l'obscur de mon humanité
Par les rayons de leur jumelle flâme.

O cent fois donq & cent fois bienheureux
L'heureux aspect de mon astre amoureux!
Puis que le ciel voulut à ma naissance

Du plus divin de mes affections
Par l'allambic de voz perfections
Tirer d'Amour une cinquiesme essence.

That Paradise, that with each sigh will strew
Saintly, angelic balm, smiles wide the gate,
Open unto the heavenly estate
Where swoons my godly spirit, drawn thereto.

Those two suns, torches for my soul, shine through
My being: their twin flames' rays pierce, penetrate
The human darkness of my mortal fate,
That I might grant Divinity its due.

O star of love, that twice a hundredfold
Shines on me with its happy mien! Behold!
For at my birth it was the powers above

That bade me, by your perfect alchemy,
Distill my passion pure, most heavenly,
Into the quintessential draught of Love.

XIII Sonnetz de l'honneste amour, V

This is where love & heaven are brought together

LES ANTIQUITEZ DE ROME

Nouveau venu, qui cherches Rome en Rome
Et rien de Rome en Rome n'apperçois,★
Ces vieux palais, ces vieux arcz que tu vois,
Et ces vieux murs, c'est ce que Rome on nomme.

Voy quel orgueil, quelle ruine: & comme
Celle qui mist le monde sous ses loix,
Pour donter tout, se donta quelquefois,
Et devint proye au temps, qui tout consomme.

Rome de Rome est le seul monument,
Et Rome Rome a vaincu seulement.†
Le Tybre seul, qui vers la mer s'enfuit,

Reste de Rome. O mondaine inconstance!
Ce qui est ferme, est par le temps destruit,
Et ce qui fuit, au temps fait resistance.

★*Les Antiquitez de Rome* (1558) conjures up the past grandeur of the
city from which Renaissance humanists drew their inspiration. In his *My-
thologies,* Fulgentius advanced the theory that *nomen est omen,* that is, that
names foretell the fate of their bearers. Du Bellay inherits the belief that
names have the power of incantation. The *Antiquitez* is one of four collec-
tions Du Bellay published upon return from his sojourn in Rome as secre-
tary to his cousin, Cardinal Jean Du Bellay. [HG]
    †Rome is the exemplary case of time's destruction, interpreted in the
moral sense of the arrogance that propelled Rome to its own downfall. [HG]

Stranger, who look for Rome in Rome, but find
Little of what was Rome in Rome, behold!
Those arches, walls, and palaces of old
Are all that Rome, in name, has left behind.

Proud ruins She, who had all humankind
Under her laws' dominion long controlled,
Through victories and victories untold,
Perished, to all-consuming Time consigned.

Rome is Rome's final lasting monument,
And Rome, Rome's one last conquest, power-spent;
Only the Tiber, flowing toward the sea,

Remains of Rome! O man's fate, constant never!
Time wastes what changeless seems, stands solidly;
The fleeting conquers time, flows on forever.

Les Antiquitez de Rome, III

Des Antiquites,
Le troisiesme liure translaté
d'italien en franchois.

ROMA QVANTA FVIT IPSA RVINA DOCET

Sacrez costaux, & vous sainctes ruines,
Qui le seul nom de Rome retenez,
Vieux monuments, qui encor soustenez
L'honneur poudreux de tant d'ames divines:

Arcz triomphaux, pointes du ciel voisines,
Qui de vous voir le ciel mesme estonnez,
Las, peu à peu cendre vous devenez,
Fable du peuple & publiques rapines!

Et bien qu'au temps pour un temps facent guerre
Les bastimens, si est-ce que le temps
Œuvres & noms finablement atterre.

Tristes desirs, vivez donques contents:
Car si le temps finist chose si dure,
Il finira la peine que j'endure.

You sacred ruins, soon to turn to dust,
You sacred hills, remnants of Rome's demise,
Old monuments wherein, still living, lies
The honored ash of many a soul august:

Triumphal arches, obelisks that thrust
Your points unto the disbelieving skies,
Spurned by the common folk who scorn, despise
And plunder you to feed their vulgar lust!

And though the buildings for a time wage war
On Time itself, Time finally conquers all,
Burying names and works that are no more.

Sad yearnings mine! Live on, content withal:
If Time lays waste such solid things, just so
Will it consume the pains that lay me low.

Les Antiquitez de Rome, VII

Mars vergongneux d'avoir donné tant d'heur
A ses nepveux,★ que l'impuissance humaine
Enorgueillie en l'audace Romaine
Sembloit fouler la celeste grandeur,

Refroidissant ceste premiere ardeur,
Dont le Romain avoit l'ame si pleine,
Soufla son feu, & d'une ardente haleine
Vint eschauffer la Gottique froideur.

Ce peuple adonc, nouveau fils de la Terre,†
Dardant par tout les fouldres de la guerre,
Ces braves murs accabla sous sa main,

Puis se perdit dans le sein de sa mere,
Afin que nul, fust-ce des Dieux le pere,
Se peust vanter de l'empire Romain.

★Mars is, of course, the father of Romulus, the ancestor of the Romans.
[HG]
    †The people in question are the giants, the race that challenged the gods
for supremacy. [HG]

Ashamed that he had shown his progeny—
Man's feeble race—so much good chance that they,
With Rome's audacity, seemed to display
An utter scorn for heaven's majesty,

Mars, cooling all the martial zeal that he
Had breathed into Rome's soul, cast it away,
And, with a gust of fiery breath, one day,
Heated to flame the Goths' frigidity:

That race, Earth's newborn sons, now more and more
Hurling about the thunderbolts of war,
Turned these fine walls into a catacomb,

Then vanished in their mother's breast, mere ghost,
Lest any, even Jupiter, should boast
Of laying waste the glory that was Rome.

Les Antiquitez de Rome, XI

Tout le parfait dont le ciel nous honnore,
Tout l'imparfait qui naist dessous les cieux,
Tout ce qui paist noz esprits & noz yeux,
Et tout cela qui noz plaisirs devore:

Tout le malheur qui nostre aage dedore,
Tout le bon heur des siecles les plus vieux,
Rome du temps de ses premiers ayeux
Le tenoit clos, ainsi qu'une Pandore.

Mais le Destin débrouillant ce Chaos,
Ou tout le bien & le mal fut enclos,
A fait depuis que les vertus divines

Volant au ciel ont laissé les pechez,
Qui jusq' icy se sont tenus cachez
Sous les monceaux de ces vieilles ruines.

Everything perfect, heaven's gift to us;
Everything less than perfect here below;
Everything that our eyes, our minds, can know,
And that turns pleasure dull and dolorous:

Everything that bespeaks ills odious;
Everything fortune-touched, spawned long ago:
All of this Rome contained—Time's weal, Time's woe—
As did Pandora's box, the infamous.

But Fate, at length, that Chaos has disposed,
Where good and ill, enmingled, lay enclosed,
And virtues, godlike, to the heavens have flown,

Leaving behind the sin, the woe, the bane,
That, until now, untouched, have hidden lain
Beneath these ruins' heaps of ancient stones.

Les Antiquitez de Rome, XIX

Toy qui de Rome emerveillé contemples
L'antique orgueil, qui menassoit les cieux,
Ces vieux palais, ces monts audacieux,
Ces murs, ces arcz, ces thermes & ces temples,

Juge, en voyant ces ruines si amples,
Ce qu'a rongé le temps injurieux,
Puis qu'aux ouvriers les plus industrieux
Ces vieux fragmens encor servent d'exemples.

Regarde apres, comme de jour en jour
Rome fouillant son antique sejour,
Se rebatist de tant d'œuvres divines:

Tu jugeras que le dæmon Romain
S'efforce encor d'une fatale main
Ressusciter ces poudreuses ruines.

You who, beholding Rome with awestruck eye,
Gaze at what once she was—those temples, those
Palaces, arches, baths, those hills that rose,
Arrogantly, against the very sky—

Judge, as you view them, how naught can defy
Time and the cruel destruction that it sows,
Mourning, like craftsman who, though zealous, knows
One day his work in rubble too will lie.

Then look again, and judge how, each day, Rome,
Delving within what was her ancient home,
Rebuilds herself in glorious opulence;

How Rome's soul, at fate's urging, takes great pains
To raise from dust her crumbled, dead remains,
And breathe to life her past magnificence.

Les Antiquitez de Rome, XXVII

Esperez vous que la posterité
Doive (mes vers) pour tout jamais vous lire?
Esperez vous que l'œuvre d'une lyre
Puisse acquerir telle immortalité?

Si sous le ciel fust quelque eternité,
Les monuments que je vous ay fait dire,
Non en papier, mais en marbre & porphyre,
Eussent gardé leur vive antiquité.

Ne laisse pas toutefois de sonner,
Luth, qu'Apollon m'a bien daigné donner:
Car si le temps ta gloire ne desrobbe,

Vanter te peux, quelque bas que tu sois,
D'avoir chanté, le premier des François,
L'antique honneur du peuple à longue robbe.

poets wish for infamy

Do you hope, O you verses mine, to be
Still read by our posterity forever?
Do you hope that a lyre's noble endeavor
Can earn such fame immortal, endlessly?

If things could last, eternal, we should see
Those monuments I sing still standing ever:
Not paper monuments, but, aging never,
Solid, of marble and of porphyry.

Hush not, however, O my lute, obtained
From god Apollo, who it was that deigned
Grant me your art; for if time spares your glory,

Well may you boast that you were first among
The French—though low your station—to have sung
The ancients', toga-clad, heroic story.

Les Antiquitez de Rome, XXXII

LES REGRETS

A son livre★

Mon livre (& je ne suis sur ton aise envieux)
Tu t'en iras sans moy voir la Court de mon Prince.†
He chetif que je suis, combien en gré je prinsse
Qu'un heur pareil au tien fust permis à mes yeux!

Là si quelqu'un vers toy se monstre gracieux,
Souhaite luy qu'il vive heureux en sa province:
Mais si quelque malin obliquement te pince,
Souhaite luy tes pleurs & mon mal ennuieux.

Souhaite luy encor' qu'il face un long voyage,
Et bien qu'il ait de veüe elongné son mesnage,
Que son cueur, ou qu'il voise, y soit tousjours present:

★This is the third of three liminary pieces introducing the collection *Les Regrets,* published in 1558, the same year as *Les Antiquitez de Rome,* the *Poemata,* and the *Divers Jeux rustiques.* (The first is a brief "To the Reader" in Latin; the second is a lengthy twenty-seven-quatrain complaint addressed to the French ambassador to the Holy See, one Jean de Saint-Marcel, seigneur d'Avanson, voicing in general the theme that the collection would explore in detail.) Du Bellay remained in Rome until August 1557, after which he returned to France, where he died in 1560. [HG]

†The prince alluded to is Henri II, who was to die in 1559 as the result of a wound he suffered while jousting in a tournament. [HG]

To His Book

O book of mine (let me not envious be!),
Off will you fly to see my Prince, whilst I
Must, luckless, languish here, alone! Ah, why
May not my eyes share your fair destiny!

To such at Court as treats you graciously,
Wish a long, happy life, forever nigh
His hearth; but if one handle you awry,
Wish him your tears and my fell misery;

Wish him a journey far from home as well,
And, in whatever climes he chance to dwell,
Let homeward yearning grieve his heart and mind;

Souhaite qu'il vieillisse en longue servitude,
Qu'il n'esprouve à la fin que toute ingratitude,
Et qu'on mange son bien pendant qu'il est absent.

Wish him a servile, toadying old age
With foul ingratitude his only wage,
And knaves to waste what wealth he leaves behind.

Les Regrets

Je ne veulx point fouiller au sein de la nature,
Je ne veulx point chercher l'esprit de l'univers,
Je ne veulx point sonder les abysmes couvers,
Ny desseigner du ciel la belle architecture.

Je ne peins mes tableaux de si riche peinture,
Et si hauts argumens ne recherche à mes vers:
Mais suivant de ce lieu les accidents divers,
Soit de bien, soit de mal, j'escris à l'adventure.★

Je me plains à mes vers, si j'ay quelque regret:
Je me ris avec eulx, je leur dy mon secret,
Comme estans de mon cœur les plus seurs secretaires.

Aussi ne veulx-je tant les pigner & friser,
Et de plus braves noms ne les veulx deguiser
Que de papiers journaux ou bien de commentaires.

★The phrase "accidents divers" submits writing to an aesthetic of chance, sustained by the notion of "l'adventure"—etymologically, "what comes" to mind or what happens unexpectedly. In other words, Du Bellay is not tethered to lofty themes that traditionally define the preoccupations of poets. His frequent use of anaphora, typically in the negative, declares his independence from predecessors. [HG]

I do not wish to probe the stars' intent,
I do not wish to fathom nature's breast,
I do not wish to plumb the deeps, or wrest
Its cosmic workings from the firmament.

My brush paints not in colors opulent,
Nor is my verse of noble aims possessed:
For good or ill, I write as suits me best,
Of paltry fact and petty incident.

My verse is my true confidant: I share
With it my heart's regrets and head's despair;
I laugh with it, trust it my confidences.

But coif it will I not, embellish it,
Or call it more than what it is: to wit,
Diaries, tracts, devoid of consequences.

Les Regrets, I

Las, ou est maintenant ce mespris de Fortune?
Ou est ce cœur vainqueur de toute adversité,
Cest honneste desir de l'immortalité,
Et ceste honneste flamme au peuple non commune?

Ou sont ces doulx plaisirs, qu'au soir soubs la nuict brune
Les Muses me donnoient, alors qu'en liberté
Dessus le verd tapy d'un rivage esquarté
Je les menois danser aux rayons de la Lune?

Maintenant la Fortune est maistresse de moy,
Et mon cœur, qui souloit estre maistre de soy,
Est serf de mille maux & regrets qui m'ennuyent.

De la posterité je n'ay plus de souci,
Ceste divine ardeur, je ne l'ay plus aussi,
Et les Muses de moy, comme estranges, s'enfuyent.*

*Du Bellay introduces the theme of exile expressed in the loss of inspiration. The Roman poet Ovid was exiled to the Black Sea, and it is the collection he wrote there, *Tristia,* that furnished the model for elegiac poetry in the Renaissance. The Angevin poet experienced his years in Rome as an exile from his *foyer* (hearth) of Anjou. [HG]

Alas, where is that scorn I used to show
For Fortune? Where, my all-victorious heart?
My <u>dream to vanquish time with timeless art?</u>
That inner fire that few will ever know?

Where, the delights the Muses would bestow
Upon me, when, in shadows, we would start
Our nightly greensward revels, set apart
At river's edge, by moonlight's gentle glow?

Now Fortune treats me as her whim demands;
Today my heart, once its own master, stands
In thrall to woes, regrets, a thousandfold.

I care not for posterity's acclaim;
Within me burns no more the sacred flame:
The Muses flee from me, grown silent, cold.

Les Regrets, VI

France, mere des arts, des armes & des loix,
Tu m'as nourry long temps du laict de ta mamelle:
Ores, comme un aigneau qui sa nourrisse appelle,
Je remplis de ton nom les antres & les bois.

Si tu m'as pour enfant advoué quelquefois,
Que ne me respons-tu maintenant, ô cruelle?
France, France, respons à ma triste querelle.
Mais nul, sinon Echo, ne respond à ma voix.

Entre les loups cruels j'erre parmy la plaine,
Je sens venir l'hyver, de qui la froide haleine
D'une tremblante horreur fait herisser ma peau.

Las, tes autres aigneaux n'ont faute de pasture,
Ils ne craignent le loup, le vent ny la froidure:
Si ne suis-je pourtant le pire du troppeau.

France, mother of arts, of laws, of soldiery,
Long did your bosom suckle me; now I,
Like lamb ripped from the teat, do vainly cry
Your name through woods and glens: come succor me!

If once I was your child, why, suddenly,
Must you, grown heartless now, make no reply?
France, France, give ear: hear, hear my plaintive sigh.
Alas, Echo alone answers my plea.

Over the plain, midst vicious wolves I go;
I feel the winter's breath: soon will it blow
Its gusts, and I will shudder, terror-cursed.

But why? Your other lambs browse, graze their fill,   *pastoral*
And fear nor wolf, nor wind, nor winter's chill.
Yet am I not, of all your flock, the worst.

Les Regrets, IX

Si celuy qui s'appreste à faire un long voyage
Doit croire cestuy là qui a ja voyagé,
Et qui des flots marins longuement oultragé,
Tout moite & degoutant s'est sauvé du naufrage,

Tu me croiras (Ronsard) bien que tu sois plus sage,
Et quelque peu encor (ce croy-je) plus aagé,★
Puis que j'ay devant toy en ceste mer nagé,
Et que desja ma nef descouvre le rivage.

Donques je t'advertis que ceste mer Romaine,
De dangereux escueils & de bancs toute pleine,
Cache mille perils, & qu'icy bien souvent

Trompé du chant pippeur des monstres de Sicile,
Pour Charybde eviter tu tomberas en Scylle,†
Si tu ne sçais nager d'une voile à tout vent.

★Du Bellay's assertion here casts doubt on the exact year of his birth, variously given as 1522, 1524, and 1525, and his parenthetical "ce croy-je" (I think so) would suggest that even he himself was not too sure. The year generally accepted by most creditable scholars, however, is 1522. [NRS]

†Like so many humanist writers, including François Rabelais, Du Bellay alludes to the *Adages* (1500–1536), a trove of ancient proverbs assembled by the Dutch humanist Erasmus, from which he drew examples. Here, Du Bellay recalls *Adages* 1.5.4: *Evitata Charybdi in Scyllam incidi* (fall from Charybdis into Scylla, or fall from a bad thing into a worse). The treacherous whirlpool is found in Homer's *Odyssey* and later identified with the Straits of Messina. [HG]

If he who readies now to set sail for
Far-distant climes would but pay heed to one
Who, long by storm and swelling surge undone,
Survived his shipwreck, drenched, wracked to the core,

Then, wiser far than I, and somewhat more
Advanced in years, Ronsard, you will not shun
My word: my course, long before yours begun,
Is over, and my bark returns to shore.

Thus would I warn you that this Roman sea
Conceals a myriad reefs, shoals, treacherously;
And that, unless your sail be stout and sure,

Gulled by Sicilian monsters' siren-call,
Fleeing Charybdis, often will you fall,
Instead, into fell Scylla's deadly lure.

Les Regrets, XXVI

Heureux qui, comme Ulysse, a fait un beau voyage,
Ou comme cestuy là qui conquit la toison,
Et puis est retourné, plein d'usage & raison,
Vivre entre ses parents le reste de son aage!

Quand revoiray-je, helas, de mon petit village
Fumer la cheminee, & en quelle saison
Revoiray-je le clos de ma pauvre maison,
Qui m'est une province, & beaucoup d'avantage?

Plus me plaist le sejour qu'ont basty mes ayeux,
Que des palais Romains le front audacieux:
Plus que le marbre dur me plaist l'ardoise fine,

Plus mon Loyre Gaulois que le Tybre Latin,
Plus mon petit Lyré que le mont Palatin,★
Et plus que l'air marin la doulceur Angevine.

★The small Anjou town of Liré, in the valley of the Loire, was Du Bellay's
birthplace. [NRS]

Happy the man who, like Ulysses, went
Sailing afar; or him who won the fleece,
Then, wise and worldly grown, returned to Greece,
Amongst his own, to live and die content.

Alas! When shall I end my banishment,
To see my village rooftops smoke, to cease
My wandering, see my humble home, in peace,
More grand to me than realm magnificent?

More do I love the home my fathers made
Than Rome's bold palaces, in pride arrayed:
More do I love fine slate than marble rare;

More than their Tiber do I love my Loire;
Their Palatine, more my Liré by far;
And more than sea's salt breeze, Anjou's soft air.

Les Regrets, XXXI

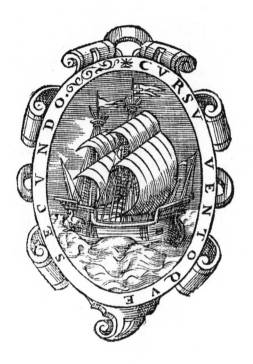

Je me feray sçavant en la philosophie,
En la mathematique & medicine aussi:
Je me feray legiste, & d'un plus hault souci
Apprendray les secrets de la theologie:

Du lut & du pinceau j'esbateray ma vie,
De l'escrime & du bal. Je discourois ainsi,
Et me vantois en moy d'apprendre tout cecy,
Quand je changeay la France au sejour d'Italie.

O beaux discours humains! je suis venu si loing,
Pour m'enrichir d'ennuy, de vieillesse & de soing,
Et perdre en voyageant le meilleur de mon aage.

Ainsi le marinier souvent pour tout tresor
Rapporte des harencs en lieu de lingots d'or,
Ayant fait, comme moy, un malheureux voyage.*

*Note the echo of Sonnet XXXI, line 1, in the final line of this poem. The contrast between the poet's "fruitless" voyage and Ulysses' happy one provides a chain of allusion, or *guirlande,* to structure the theme of nostalgia (Sonnets XXV–XXXVI) expressed in the recurring motif of navigation. [HG]

"In mathematics and philosophy,
In medicine and law, will I acquire
Great knowledge, and more loftily aspire
To learn the secrets of theology;

"Of duel and dance will I gain mastery,
And cheer my days with skill of brush and lyre."
So did I boast, imbued with learning's fire,
When I quit France in quest of Italy.

Oh, what fine human words! Far did I come
To reap a store of woe and tedium,
And in my travels grow untimely old.

Thus often does the traveler, treasure-bent,
Return from voyage fruitless and ill-spent,
Laden with herring though he sought for gold.

Les Regrets, XXXII

Comme le marinier, que le cruel orage
A long temps agité dessus la haulte mer,
Ayant finablement à force de ramer
Garanty son vaisseau du danger du naufrage,

Regarde sur le port, sans plus craindre la rage
Des vagues ny des vents, les ondes escumer:
Et quelqu'autre bien loing, au danger d'abysmer,
En vain tendre les mains vers le front du rivage:

Ainsi (mon cher Morel) sur le port arresté★
Tu regardes la mer, & vois en seureté
De mille tourbillons son onde renversee:

Tu la vois jusqu'au ciel s'eslever bien souvent,
Et vois ton Dubellay à la mercy du vent
Assis au gouvernail dans une nef persee.

★As he does in many of *Les Regrets,* Du Bellay is here apostrophizing a
friend; in this case Jean Morel, native of Embrun, *gentilhomme* in service to
Catherine de Médicis, wife of Henri II, who succeeded his father, Fran-
çois I. Morel was especially influential in his early support of Ronsard.
[NRS]

Like seaman caught up in the storm, pell–mell,
Plying the sea, dark ocean deep and vast,
Who, strong of oar and stout of arm, at last
Rescues his vessel from the deadly swell;

Who looks to shore, fears now no tempest fell,
Saved from the storm, for him now safely past;
Then sees, afar, another, sinking fast,
Arms stretched, in vain, toward port; my dear Morel,

You watch the sea in safety from the shore,
The swirling sea, buffeted more and more,
Its myriad whirlpools rising fore and aft,

Reaching almost to heaven; and you see
Your Du Bellay, lashed by the wind, as he
Sits at the rudder of a leaking craft.

Les Regrets, **XXXIV**

[handwritten annotation: using his own name — makes him stand out from the rest of the poem]

O qu'heureux est celuy qui peult passer son aage
Entre pareils à soy! & qui sans fiction,
Sans crainte, sans envie & sans ambition,
Regne paisiblement en son pauvre mesnage!

Le miserable soing d'acquerir d'avantage
Ne tyrannise point sa libre affection,
Et son plus grand desir, desir sans passion,
Ne s'estend plus avant que son propre heritage.

Il ne s'empesche point des affaires d'autruy,
Son principal espoir ne depend que de luy,
Il est sa court, son roy, sa faveur & son maistre.

Il ne mange son bien en païs estranger,
Il ne met pour autruy sa personne en danger,
Et plus riche qu'il est ne voudroit jamais estre.

O happy he, whose latter years are spent
Amongst his own, his intimates! who, free
Of lies, of fear, of jealous enmity,
Reigns in his humble dwelling, calm, content!

The base desire more and more opulent
To grow holds not his soul in thrall; for he
Sagely accepts what largesse destiny
Sees fit to grant him in his line's descent.

He troubles not with others' power or pelf,
His hopes depend on him alone, himself,
He, his own court, king, patron, master is;

He wastes his fortune not on foreign soil,
He risks not harm for others' toil and moil,
And seeks no greater wealth than what is his.

Les Regrets, XXXVIII

Je n'escris point d'amour, n'estant point amoureux,
Je n'escris de beauté, n'ayant belle maistresse,
Je n'escris de douceur, n'esprouvant que rudesse,
Je n'escris de plaisir, me trouvant douloureux:

Je n'escris de bon heur, me trouvant malheureux,
Je n'escris de faveur, ne voyant ma Princesse,★
Je n'escris de tresors, n'ayant point de richesse,
Je n'escris de santé, me sentant langoureux:

Je n'escris de la Court, estant loing de mon Prince,
Je n'escris de la France, en estrange province,
Je n'escris de l'honneur, n'en voyant point icy:

Je n'escris d'amitié, ne trouvant que feintise,
Je n'escris de vertu, n'en trouvant point aussi,
Je n'escris de sçavoir, entre les gens d'Eglise.

★Marguerite de France, also called Marguerite de Valois, daughter of Henri II and Catherine de Médicis, who was the poet's protector. During his Roman years (1553–1557), Du Bellay saw at first hand the decadence of the papacy under Popes Julius III and Paul IV, during whose reigns intrigue, war, and scandal prevailed. Du Bellay's melancholy originates in the disappointment that Rome's ancient greatness, a beacon for humanists, had devolved to debauchery. The satire of Rome dominates in *Les Regrets,* LXXVIII–CXXII. [HG]

I sing not love, for I feel not a whit;
I sing not beauty, mistress none have I;
I sing not kindness, harshly used, awry;
I sing not pleasure, knowing none of it;

I sing not luck, possessing not one bit;
I sing not grace, my Princess dwells not nigh;
I sing not wealth, for naught have I put by;
I sing not health, grown weary and unfit;

I sing not Court, my Prince bides far from me;
I sing not France, exiled to Italy;
I sing not honor, seeing nor jot nor tittle;

I sing not friendship, here reigns artfulness;
I sing not virtue, here find I still less;
I sing not learning: Churchmen have but little.

Les Regrets, LXXIX

Marcher d'un grave pas & d'un grave sourci,
Et d'un grave soubriz à chascun faire feste,
Balancer tous ses mots, respondre de la teste,
Avec un *Messer non,* ou bien un *Messer si:*

Entremesler souvent un petit *Et cosi,*
Et d'un *son Servitor'* contrefaire l'honneste,
Et, comme si lon eust sa part en la conqueste,
Discourir sur Florence, & sur Naples aussi:

Seigneuriser chascun d'un baisement de main,
Et suivant la façon du courtisan Romain,
Cacher sa pauvreté d'une brave apparence:

Voila de ceste Court la plus grande vertu,
Dont souvent mal monté, mal sain, & mal vestu,
Sans barbe & sans argent on s'en retourne en France.★

★Du Bellay bemoans the fact that a severe case of alopecia, one of the physical ills that plagued him during his Roman stay—in addition to the moral ones—caused the hair on his face to fall out. Henri Chamard, in his critical edition of *Les Regrets* (2:126, note 1), cites a medical text of the period purporting to explain the condition as being related to the pox, or *la maladie néapolitaine.* [NRS]

To walk with solemn step, frown solemnly,
And greet with solemn smile each passerby,
To ponder every word, nod a reply,
Now with a *Messer non,* now *Messer si:*

To interject a little *E così,*
And with *son Servitor'* throw dust in eye,
To rant—like indispensable ally—
On Florence, Naples, war, and victory:

To fawn on one and all, hands humbly kissed,
And, like the Roman courtier, to insist
On masking penury with elegance:

Such are this Court's most noble qualities,
And thus, ill-horsed, ill-clad, racked with disease,
Beardless and beggared, one returns to France.

Les Regrets, LXXXVI

Heureux celuy qui peult long temps suivre la guerre
Sans mort, ou sans blesseure, ou sans longue prison!
Heureux qui longuement vit hors de sa maison
Sans despendre son bien ou sans vendre sa terre!

Heureux qui peult en Court quelque faveur acquerre
Sans crainte de l'envie ou de quelque traïson!
Heureux qui peult long temps sans danger de poison
Jouir d'un chapeau rouge ou des clefz de sainct Pierre!

Heureux qui sans peril peult la mer frequenter!
Heureux qui sans procez le palais peult hanter!
Heureux qui peult sans mal vivre l'aage d'un homme!

Heureux qui sans soucy peult garder son tresor,
Sa femme sans souspçon, & plus heureux encor'
Qui a peu sans peler vivre trois ans à Rome!

Happy the man who watches war at ease,
Untouched by death, or wound, or prison's chill!
Happy, who, from his home long absent, still
Can cling to all his wealth, his properties.

Happy, who, favored by the Court's grandees,
Fears not lest, envious, they will do him ill!
Happy, who, unafraid of potions, will
Wear the red cap, or bear Saint Peter's keys!

Happy, who sails without vicissitude!
Happy, who courts the Law, unscathed, unsued!
Happy, who lives man's days unmarred by care!

Happy, who keeps his treasure free of threat;
His wife, free of dishonor; happier yet,
Who spends three years in Rome, but keeps his hair!*

Les Regrets, XCIV

*See p. 223, note.

Comme un qui veult curer quelque Cloaque immunde,★
S'il n'a le nez armé d'une contresenteur,
Estouffé bien souvent de la grand'puanteur
Demeure ensevely dans l'ordure profonde:

Ainsi le bon Marcel ayant levé la bonde,
Pour laisser escouler la fangeuse espesseur
Des vices entassez, dont son predecesseur
Avoit six ans devant empoisonné le monde:†

Se trouvant le pauvret de telle odeur surpris,
Tomba mort au milieu de son œuvre entrepris,
N'ayant pas à demy ceste ordure purgee.

Mais quiconques rendra tel ouvrage parfait,
Se pourra bien vanter d'avoir beaucoup plus fait
Que celuy qui purgea les estables d'Augee.

★This poem is one of eight (*Les Regrets,* CV–CXII) that did not circulate
freely but were pasted between two pages of the first edition and destined for
the eyes of Du Bellay's friends only. They contain the fiercest criticism of the
Vatican and its scandals, including allusions to Pope Julius III's alleged sod-
omy. For the editorial history, see Chamard 2:6–8. [HG]

†The references are to the well-intentioned Pope Marcellus II, who died
in 1555 after a pontificate of only twenty-one days, and his less-than-
exemplary predecessor, Julius III. [NRS]

Like one who would drain clean a Gutter vile,
But, wearing on his nose no guarantor
Against the stench, chokes amid fumes galore,
Buried deep in the fetid muck the while,

So good Marcellus tried, pope free of guile,
To purge the filth that he who reigned before,
In six vice-stinking years, each one the more,
Heaped on a suffering world, pile upon pile.

The poor soul, by the squalor stunned and shaken,
Died, scarcely had the charge been undertaken;
And still the swill lay foul, and thick, and deep.

Ah! He who would this task do properly
Must labor more than did that deity
Who the Augean stables had to sweep.

Les Regrets, CIX

Si tu veulx seurement en Court te maintenir,★
Le silence (Ronsard) te soit comme un decret.
Qui baille à son amy la clef de son secret,
Le fait de son amy son maistre devenir.

Tu dois encor' (Ronsard) ce me semble, tenir
Aveq' ton ennemy quelque moyen discret,
Et faisant contre luy, monstrer qu'à ton regret
Le seul devoir te fait en ces termes venir.

Nous voyons bien souvent une longue amitié
Se changer pour un rien en fiere inimitié,
Et la haine en amour souvent se transformer.

Dont (veu le temps qui court) il ne fault s'esbaïr.
Ayme donques (Ronsard) comme pouvant haïr,
Haïs donques (Ronsard) comme pouvant aymer.

★This sonnet belongs to the so-called Parisian sonnets (*Les Regrets,*
CXXXVIII–CXCI), whose satire is directed against the court of Henri II
and Catherine de Médicis. The fiction of return from Rome to find intrigue
in princely courts in France leads to a series of reflections on how to survive
through maneuvers of various sorts. [HG]

Ronsard, if you would hold your own at Court,
Then hold your tongue; for in such company,
When friend shares with a friend his secrets, he
Makes him his master, of most dangerous sort.

What's more, Ronsard, I hasten to exhort
That you show caution with your enemy:
Should he reprove you for your contumely,
"Alas, duty demands!" be your retort.

Often, for but a trifle, friends become
Sworn enemies; and no less often, some
Come to love whom they once would deprecate.

Ronsard, stand not, these days, in awe thereof;
Rather, prepare to hate whom first you love,
And, in like wise, to love whom first you hate.

Les Regrets, CXL

Vous dictes (Courtisans) les Poëtes sont fouls,
Et dictes verité: mais aussi dire j'ose,
Que telz que vous soyez, vous tenez quelque chose
De ceste doulce humeur qui est commune à tous.

Mais celle-là (Messieurs) qui domine sur vous,
En autres actions diversement s'expose:
Nous sommes fouls en rime, & vous l'estes en prose:
C'est le seul different qu'est entre vous & nous.

Vray est que vous avez la Court plus favorable,
Mais aussi n'avez vous un renom si durable:
Vous avez plus d'honneurs, & nous moins de souci.

Si vous riez de nous, nous faisons la pareille:
Mais cela qui se dit s'en vole par l'oreille,
Et cela qui s'escript ne se perd pas ainsi.

Poets are mad: so, Courtiers, you declare;
And right you are; but I daresay that you
Have not a little of that madness too,
That softness of the head that all men share.

If you and us, however, we compare,
Different the forms of madness we pursue:
Ours is in rhyme, and yours, in prose; though true,
No other difference 'twixt the two is there.

Your names are known at Court, hither and yon,
But your renown lasts little; ours lives on:
You have more honors; we, less bale and bane.

So twit us if you must, with chaff and sneer:
We might do likewise; for what one can hear
Blows on the wind, but written words remain.

Les Regrets, CXLIX

Seigneur, je ne sçaurois regarder d'un bon œil
Ces vieux Singes de Court, qui ne sçavent rien faire,★
Sinon en leur marcher les Princes contrefaire,
Et se vestir, comme eulx, d'un pompeux appareil.

Si leur maistre se mocque, ilz feront le pareil,
S'il ment, ce ne sont eulx qui diront du contraire,
Plustost auront-ilz veu, à fin de luy complaire,
La Lune en plein midy, à minuict le Soleil.

Si quelqu'un devant eulx reçoit un bon visage,
Ilz le vont caresser, bien qu'ilz crevent de rage:
S'il le reçoit mauvais, ilz le monstrent au doy.

Mais ce qui plus contre eulx quelquefois me despite,
C'est quand devant le Roy, d'un visage hypocrite,
Ilz se prennent à rire, & ne sçavent pourquoy.

★Monkeys symbolized hypocrites and *beaux parleurs* (slick talkers) in Du
Bellay's time. The expression *payer en monnaie de singe* (pay with monkeys'
change) is attested for the first time in 1552. [HG]

Lord, I cannot look less than loathingly
Upon these Apes at Court, old toadies who
Mimic their Prince's manners, through and through,
And clothe themselves in garish panoply.

Their lord makes sport? They do the same. If he
Speaks false, they much approve, without ado;
The Moon at noon, the Sun at midnight, too,
They swear to see, to please His Majesty.

If one be well received, with politesse,
Though they despise him, him will they caress;
If ill received, him will they vilify.

But most I loathe the manner counterfeit
In which, before the King, each hypocrite
Cackles with laughter, though he knows not why.

Les Regrets, CL

DIVERS JEUX RUSTIQUES

D'un Vanneur de blé, aux vents

A vous troppe legere,
Qui d'æle passagere
Par le monde volez,
Et d'un sifflant murmure
L'ombrageuse verdure
Doulcement esbranlez,

J'offre ces violettes,
Ces lis, & ces fleurettes,
Et ces roses icy,
Ces vermeillettes roses,
Tout freschement écloses,
Et ces œilletz aussi.*

---

*Several poems in the *Divers Jeux rustiques* practice the genre of the *vœu*, or ex-voto, derived from the ancient custom of making dedications to the gods in Greek and Roman religions. The act of giving was made publicly, sometimes entailing the gift of a statuette placed in a sanctuary. Du Bellay's simplicity here and in his poems "A Cerés" and "D'un Berger" (IV and VI) suggests the agricultural setting of Virgil's *Georgics*. [HG]

A Winnower of Wheat, to the Winds

To you, O airy band,
Blowing over the land
On gusts of fleeting wing,
Who, rustling in the shade
Of leaves, grass, softly swayed,
Are faintly murmuring,

I bring, and offer you,
Lilies, and violets too,
And even roses: these,
Fresh-bloomed and ruby red
With petals rare, outspread;
And pinks too, if you please.

De vostre doulce halaine
Eventez ceste plaine,
Eventez ce sejour:
Ce pendant que j'ahanne
A mon blé, que je vanne
A la chaleur du jour.

Blow fair and gentle, pray,
Over the plain this day,
Here, in the midday heat:
Whilst I, with every breath,
Gasping, near done to death,
Toil winnowing my wheat.

Divers Jeux rustiques, III

A Cerés, à Bacchus et à Palés★

Cerés d'espicz je couronne,
Ce pampre à Bacchus je donne,
Je donne à Palés la grande
Deux potz de laict pour offrande:
Afin que Cerés la blonde
Rende la plaine feconde,
Bacchus à la vigne rie,
Et Palés à la prairie.

★The Roman goddess Pales, less familiar to modern readers than her two
mythological colleagues, was charged with the well-being of flocks. [NRS]

For Ceres, Bacchus, and Pales

On Bacchus I bestow this vine,
On Ceres' head these grains entwine,
And on great Pales I confer
Two pots of milk to honor her:
Let Bacchus, thus, fine wine produce,
Ceres the blond, a crop profuse
Over the fair and fertile plain,
And Pales, too, in her domain.

Divers Jeux rustiques, IV

D'un Berger, à Pan

Robin par bois & campaignes,
Par boccaiges & montaignes,
Suivant naguere un taureau
Egaré de son troppeau,
D'un roc elevé regarde,
Void une biche fuyarde,
D'un dard la faict trebucher,
Trouve en l'antre d'un rocher
Les petiz fanneaux, qu'il donne
A Jannette sa mignonne:
Puis fait à ses compaignons
Un banquet d'aulx & d'oignons,
Faisant courrir par la trouppe
De vin d'Anjou mainte couppe.
Quant au reste, ô Dieu cornu,
Au croc de ce pin cogneu
Pour ton offrande j'apporte
La peau de la biche morte.

From a Shepherd, to Pan

Robin, one day a-hunting gone,
Through woods, plains, hills, vales—hither, yon—
A bull was chasing, who had wandered
Off from the herd; and as he pondered,
High on a bluff, he spied below,
Fleeing and fleet of hoof, a doe;
Brought her down with an arrow, then,
Coming upon a rocky den,
Found there her fawns, gave them straightway
To sweet Jeannette, his *bien-aimée;*
Then, for his friends, skewered the beast
With garlic, onions—ah! a feast!—
And Anjou wine, a-flowing free,
To whet their joyous revelry.
All that was left, to you I bring,
O hornèd god: an offering
Placed on your pine tree, hanging there:
The dead doe's empty hide, stripped bare.

Divers Jeux rustiques, VI

D'un Vigneron, à Bacchus

Ceste vigne tant utile,
Vigne de raysins fertile,
Tousjours coustumiere d'estre
Fidele aux vœuz de son maistre,
Ores qu'elle est bien fleurie,
Te la consacre & dedie
Thenot vigneron d'icelle.
Fay donq, Bacchus, que par elle
Ne soit trompé de l'attente
Qu'il a d'une telle plante:
Et que mon Anjou foisonne
Par tout en vigne aussi bonne.

From a Winegrower to Bacchus

Now that this shoot is blooming fine,
Heavy with grapes, this precious vine
That, ever faithful, grows until
It has fulfilled its master's will,
Thénot, who grew it, does proclaim
It consecrated to your name.
And so, O Bacchus, do your best
To see that he be not distressed;
That harvest never disenchant
The hopes he has for this fair plant;
And that as fine a vine bestrew
The vineyards of my own Anjou.

Divers Jeux rustiques, VIII

Epitaphe d'un chien★

Ce bon Hurauld, qui souloit estre
Le mignon de Jacquet son maistre,
Hurauld venu du bas Poittou
Sur les doulces rives d'Anjou,
Pour garder le troppeau champestre:

Pendant que la bande compaigne
Des autres chiens, sur la campaigne
Dormant gisoit deça, dela,
Faisant le guet sur ce bord là,
Ou Meine à Loyre s'accompaigne:

Ce bon chien sur tous chiens fidele
Defendit de la dent cruelle
Les aignelets, mais ce pendant
Il mourut en les defendant,
Digne de louange immortelle.

★The genre of the epitaph is a short poem written to be inscribed on a tomb (from the Greek *epi* [on] and *taphos* [sepulcher]). The epitaph can be solemn or fanciful, and it bears an affinity to the epigram, also intended as an inscription, whose brevity often carries a barb or satirical point at the end. Here, Du Bellay notes the greed of thieving neighbors. [HG]

Epitaph for a Dog

Hurault, that good and stalwart hound,
Jacquet's most cherished pet, who found
His way to these climes Angevin
From Bas Poitou, and who, herein,
Guarded the flocks the country round:

None of his fellow dogs would deign—
Lying about our fair terrain—
Remain awake, but slept and slept
Whilst he his watchful vigil kept,
Here, where the Loire joins with the Maine.

Faithful was he, ever defending
Lambkins from certain death impending,
Under the vicious fang; and hence,
Perished one day in their defense,
Worthy of grateful praise unending.

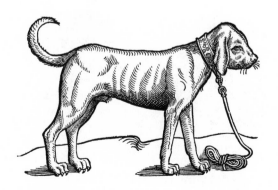

Son maistre regrettant sa perte,
L'a mis soubz ceste motte verte:
Aussi avoit bien merité
Une telle fidelité
D'estre si dignement couverte.

Les pauvres troppeaux le gemissent,
Mais les animaulx qui ravissent,
Et les larrons s'attendent bien
D'estre maistres de nostre bien,
Et de sa mort se resjouissent.

Here did his master, sore distressed
Bury him in this mound; and blessed
His loyal hound, who so well served
And tended him that he deserved
To be with honor laid to rest.

The poor flocks mourn him, moan with fright;
But the voracious beasts, who might
Now freely feed, and thieves whose stealth
Will make them masters of our wealth,
Seeing him dead, take much delight.

Divers Jeux rustiques, XI

A Venus

Ayant apres long desir
Pris de ma doulce ennemie
Quelques arres du plaisir
Que sa rigueur me denie,

Je t'offre ces beaux œillets,
Venus, je t'offre ces roses,
Dont les boutons vermeillets
Imitent les levres closes,

Que j'ay baisé par trois fois,
Marchant tout beau dessoubs l'ombre
De ce buisson, que tu vois:
Et n'ay sceu passer ce nombre,

Pource que la mere estoit
Aupres de là, ce me semble,
Laquelle nous aguettoit:
De peur encores j'en tremble.

Or' je te donne des fleurs:
Mais si tu fais ma rebelle
Autant piteuse à mes pleurs
Comme à mes yeux elle est belle,

Un Myrte je dediray
Dessus les rives de Loyre,
Et sur l'écorse escriray
Ces quatre vers à ta gloire:

THENOT SUR CE BORD ICY,
A VENUS SACRE ET ORDONNE
CE MYRTE, ET LUY DONNE AUSSI
CES TROPPEAUX ET SA PERSONNE.

To Venus

Languishing long and fruitlessly,
At length I stole from my fair foe
A token of the joys that she,
Hard-hearted wench, would not bestow.

Thus, Venus, now I bring to you
Roses and pinks, my offering,
Whose tender buds, of scarlet hue,
Are like those lips, unopening,

That thrice I kissed, here in the wood,
Hid in the shadows of this tree.
Three kisses! How I wish I could
Have kissed and kissed her endlessly:

One kiss, one more, and yet another...
But stop I did lest I be caught;
For, lurking there, I spied her mother:
Ah, how I shudder at the thought!

And so I bring you flowers. But oh!
Could you but make the heart of my
Cold wench as tender to my woe
As is her beauty to my eye,

I should a myrtle to your name
Enshrine, by river Loire, and mark
Undying homage to your fame
With these lines blazoned on its bark:

THIS TREE IN VENUS' NAME IS BLESSED
BY THENOT, SOLEMNLY DECREEING,
WHO, TO HIS GODDESS, MAKES BEQUEST
OF ALL HIS FLOCKS AND ALL HIS BEING.

Divers Jeux rustiques, XII

Estrene d'un tableau

Ce tableau, que pour t'estrener,
Isabeau, je te veux donner,
Au vif rapporte mon visage
Autant qu'on vid onques image.
Qu'ainsi soit, regarde, Isabeau,
Comme je semble à mon tableau:
La couleur du protraict est blesme,
Et la mienne est tousjours de mesme:
Sans cueur il est, sans cueur je suis,
Je n'ay point eu de cueur depuis
Qu'amour l'ostant de ma puissance,
Le meit soubs ton obeissance.
Il est muet, si suis-je moy,
Quand je me trouve devant toy.
Bref, qui nous void, voir il luy semble
Deux amans ou tableaux ensemble.
Nous sommes differents d'un poinct,
C'est qu'amour ne le brusle point.
Et quand il sentiroit la flamme,
(Comme tout par ton œil s'enflamme)
Ainsi que de moy malheureux
Son mal ne sera langoureux,
Et les flammes continuelles
Ainsi n'ardront point ses moëlles:
Au premier feu qu'il sentira,
Soudain en cendres il ira.

Gift of a Portrait

I give my portrait, Isabelle,
Herewith to you, and, truth to tell,
The image that it paints of me
Could not a truer likeness be.
Look! See how much, you must admit,
It seems like me, and I, like it,
Isabelle: pale its face and wan,
And mine as well, all color gone;
It has no heart, no heart have I,
For mine, alas! bade me good-bye
When love put me in thrall to you;
Mute is its voice, and mute mine too
When you draw near. In short, whenever
We stand together, one can never
Know if it is two lovers, or
Two portraits that one stands before.
It is, however, not a jot
Like me in one respect; for not
Is it by love inflamed; and should
It feel that fire, I know it would
Not flame with passion (that your eyes
Cast everywhere, in wanton wise),
To languish, as do I, to yearn,
And to the very marrow burn:
No; at the flame's first gentle stroke,
Lo! Watch it turn to ash and smoke.

Divers Jeux rustiques, XIII

LES AMOURS

Vous avez bien cest' angelicque face,★
Ce front serein & ces celestes yeulx
Que Laure avoit, & si avez bien mieux
Portant le nom d'une plus noble race.

Mais je n'ay pas ceste divine grace,
Ces haults discours, ces traicts ingenieux,
Qu'avoit Petrarque, & moins audacieux
Mon vol aussi tire une aile plus basse.

Pourquoy de moy avous donc souhaitté
D'estre sacree à l'immortalité,
Si vostre nom d'un seul Petrarque est digne?

Je ne sçay pas d'ou vient ce desir là,
Fors qu'il vous plaist nous monstrer par cela
Que d'un Corbeau vous pouvez faire un Cygne.

★Citing the work of Robert V. Merrill ("Considerations on *Les Amours* de J. du Bellay," *Modern Philology* 33 [1935–1936], 129–138), the Chamard edition of Du Bellay's *Œuvres poétiques* (2:322) indicates that the inspiration of the twenty-nine sonnets in this posthumous collection was probably Diane de France. The daughter of Henri II, she was the wife of Orazio Farnèse, duc de Castro, and subsequently of François de Montmorency. [NRS]

reference to Petrarch?

Yours is that angel's face, those heavenly eyes,
That brow serene, that Laura had; and more,
Although a high and stately name she bore,
Yours, nobler still, her noble name outvies.

But mine is not that grace divine; likewise
Not mine, those fine and clever traits galore
That Petrarch penned; nor can my spirit soar
On wings too weak to lift it to the skies.

How, then, do I deserve to be the one
You would have sing your deathless fame, if none
But Petrarch ought his praise on you bestow?

I know not whence may come that wish, unless
It be to show the world with what largesse
You would make me a Swan, though but a Crow.

                                        Les Amours, X

Voyez, Amants, comment ce petit Dieu
Traicte noz cueurs. Sur la fleur de mon âge,
Amour tout seul regnoit en mon courage,
Et n'y avoit la raison point de lieu.

Puis quand cest âge, augmentant peu à peu,
Vint sur ce poinct ou l'homme est le plus sage,
D'autant qu'en moy croissoit sens & usage,
D'autant aussi decroissoit ce doux feu.

Ores mes ans tendans sur la vieillesse,
(Voyez comment la raison nous delaisse)
Plus que jamais je sens ce feu d'Amour.

L'ombre au matin nous voyons ainsi croistre,
Sur le midy plus petite apparoistre,
Puis s'augmenter devers la fin du jour.

See, Lovers, how capricious is that child,
God Cupid; how he treats our hearts! When in
The bloom of youth, never could I have been
Ruled by another: reason fled, exiled.

But as time passed, and as age heaped and piled
Its years upon me, though I would begin
To grow in wisdom and mind's discipline,
Lo! As I aged, that passion-fire grew mild.

gaining reason

Now, in my waning years, as I wax old—
Ah, how cool reason looses fast its hold!—
More even than before I burn with love.

Thus do dawn's shadows that the sun casts, long,
Grow short by noon; but then, come evensong,
They lengthen with the darkling skies above.

Les Amours, XIV

SONNETS DIVERS

En la fureur de sa fiévre*

Ce Montgibel, qu'horrible je degorge,
Et ce Caucase englacé de froideur,
Ont engendré la forcenante ardeur
Qui boult, qui fume en l'antre de ma gorge.

Là je retrempe & retourne & reforge
Mille sanglots, dont l'effroyable horreur
Emmasse, entourne, endouble la fureur
De ces gros vers batus à triple forge.

Ores le feu m'est aux veines enclos,
Ores le froid me saccage les os.
Horreur, horreur, je sens dans mes entrailles

Ramper l'ardeur du maugreant Thebain:
Horreur, je sens tournasser en mon sein
De cent fureurs les mordantes tenailles.

*This and the succeeding poems were all published posthumously. [NRS]

In the Madness of His Fever

This boiling, fuming Etna,★ noxiously
Spewing forth from my throat; this Caucasus
Frigidly clutching my esophagus,
Have spawned my bosom's torrid agony.

The fever racks, and hacks, and harrows me;
Sobs puke a thousandfold their hideous
Horrors, their tortuous and torturous
Vermin, massed thick in vile immensity.

Now will fire flame within my veins; now will
Ice freeze my marrow with its deadly chill.
Horror of horrors! In my belly spreads

That heat that Nessus' tunic cruelly pressed
About poor Hercules.† Ah! In my breast
Hundreds of pincers grip, rip me to shreds.

Sonnets divers, VII

★For several centuries Mount Etna was known also as Monte Gibello.
[NRS]
†The "disgruntled Theban" ("maugreant Thebain") was Hercules, who,
having punished the centaur Nessus for offenses against him and his wife
Déjanira, suffered the centaur's revenge that led to the deaths of Hercules and
Déjanira. [NRS]

A son luth

Luth qui soulois adoucir les ennuis
Qu'ores le sort qui me tournoit sans cesse,
Ores l'amour d'une belle maistresse
M'a fait souvent souspirer jours & nuicts:

Puis que sans toy, Luth, vivre je ne puis,
Comme tu as consolé ma jeunesse,
Console aussi, je te pry, ma vieillesse,
M'ostant l'ardeur de la fiévre ou je suis.

Si tu me fais ce bien, pour recompense,
Quand cest esprit (qui doit, comme je pense,
Pour vivre au ciel, bien tost partir d'icy)

Pres d'Apollon ira prendre sa place,
Je te promets de te planter aussi
Au pres du luth du grand prestre de Thrace.

To His Lute

O Lute that once would soothe and ease the blight
Upon my soul, when love of mistress fair
Or hostile fate would rack me with despair,
Sighing my misery by day, by night:

Without you, Lute, deadly would be my plight;
As once you calmed my youth, now ease the care
Of these my waning years: hear, heed my prayer,
Quell fever's flames that my poor flesh ignite.

I promise that, if you grant me this boon,
When flies my soul (as, surely, it will soon
Depart these climes, in heaven's height to dwell)

To life eternal by Apollo's side,
You, O my Lute, shall I place there as well,
Beside the lute that Orpheus sanctified.

Sonnets divers, IX

De la saignee qui luy osta la fiévre

Si ceste pasle & vieille rechignee,
Cruelle Fiévre, horreur des siecles vieux,
Par les Romains mise au nombre des Dieux,
Sur leurs autels eust sa place assignee,

Pourquoy de nous seras-tu dedaignee,
Toy seule clef du thresor precieux
Que la santé nous apporte des cieux,
O bonne, ô saincte, ô divine Saignee?

Tu as chassé de mes os la froideur,
Tu as esteint de mes veines l'ardeur,
Tu as repeint l'honneur de mon visage:

Tu as refait la force de mes bras,
Tu as r'assis la marche de mes pas,
Tu m'as rendu la force & le courage.

Of the Bleeding That Cured His Fever

If Fever, that old, callous crone malign,
Horror of ages past, was nonetheless
Blessed with the mark of Roman godliness,
Given her altar and her holy shrine,

Why should we scorn you, who by heaven's design
Bring us the miracle of your largesse,
Return our health when direst our distress,
O worthy Bleeding, you, O cure divine?

You have cast from my bones the fell chilblains,
You have put out the fire that burned my veins,
You have retinged my cheeks their honest hue:

You have put vigor in my arms once more,
You have restored the step I had before,
You have redeemed my strength, borne me anew.

Sonnets divers, X

A Madame Marguerite★

Bien que de Mars le dedaigneux orgueil,
Bien que le feu que Cupidon attise,
Bien que de l'or l'infame convoitise
Ait mis l'honneur des lettres au cercueil:

Si ne croiray-je un eternel sommeil
Devoir presser si louable entreprise,
Tant que la fleur, que le ciel favorise,
Nous daignera contempler d'un bon œil.

Voyla pourquoy, quelque vent qui s'appreste,
Je ne crains point l'horreur de la tempeste,
Ny des rochers le dangereux abbord:

Puis que vostre œil, seul Phare de nostre age,
Au plus obscur du perilleux orage
Guigne ma nef pour la tirer au port.

★Du Bellay, as other examples have shown, was no less an admirer and adulator of Marguerite de Navarre, to whom this sonnet is written, than were the other poets and intellectuals of the age. For an example from the pen of Marot, see pp. 108–109. [NRS]

To Madame Marguerite

Though Mars' haughty disdain and martial scorn,
Though passion planted by young Cupid's dart,
Though the vile love of gold, that rules the heart,
Have, to the grave, the pride of letters borne:

Yet will I not believe it time to mourn
The endless sleep of our much honored art
So long as heaven's flower, blooming apart,
Has not her high regard for us forsworn.

And that is why, fierce though the tempest blow,
I dread nor wind, nor wave, above, below,
Nor fear to founder on the rock-bound shore:

Your eye, sole Beacon of our age, will guide
My bark, however perilous the tide
Or dark the storm, and lead it home once more.

Sonnets divers, XIX

Sur la mort de la jeunesse françoise

Que n'ay-je encor' la voix qui plus hault tonne
Le bruit de ceux qui d'un cœur indonté,
Pour maintenir la Grecque liberté,
Firent rougir les champs de Marathonne?★

Tout ce grand rond, que la mer environne,
Oyroit sonner par l'immortalité
La hardiesse & la fidelité,
Qui ont servi la Françoise couronne.

Jeunesse heureuse, heureuse pour jamais,
Nous, noz enfans, noz nepveus, desormais
Te nommerons l'honneur de ta province,

Et si dirons que ton sang espandu
Ne pouvoit pas estre mieux despendu
Qu'en soustenant le droict d'un si bon Prince.†

★Classical scholars and athletes will appreciate Du Bellay's allusion to Marathon, scene of the celebrated victory of the Greek general Miltiades over the Persians in 490 B.C.E., reported in Athens by a fleet-footed messenger who ran twenty-six miles and 385 yards (or so we are told) from the battlefield to the city. [NRS]

†The reference is to Henri II, son of François I, who continued his father's war against Charles V and Philip II of Spain and their English allies. The bloodshed referred to in lines 12–14 evokes the state of war in the 1550s that worsened when the Spanish army crushed the French at Saint-Quentin (August 1557), but then suffered a setback when François de Guise prevented the English from taking possession of Calais. The hostilities ended with the Treaty of Cateau-Cambrésis in April 1559, approximately eighteen months after Du Bellay's departure from Rome. [HG]

On the Death of French Youth

Why have I not the voice of bards long gone,
Who loudly sang the heroes' hearts of those
Who, struggling for Greek liberty, arose
And bloodied red the plains of Marathon?

About this sea-girt globe, endlessly on,
Would one hear sung the debt the French crown owes
Those stalwarts who, immortal, faced our foes,
Each one a bold and loyal paragon.

O youth, yours a most glorious destiny:
We, and our children, and their progeny
Ever your nation's gratitude will sing;

And we shall tell how your blood, nobly spread,
Never could be for worthier reason shed
Than in the cause of such a gracious King.

Sonnets divers, LII

Pierre de Ronsard

(1524 – 1585)

Le Premier Livre des Amours
Le Second Livre des Amours
Sonnets et madrigals pour Astree
Le Premier Livre des Sonnets pour Hélène
Le Second Livre des Sonnets pour Hélène
Les Amours diverses
Gayetez
Livret de folastries
Le Premier Livre des Odes
Le Second Livre des Odes
Le Quatriesme Livre des Odes
Le Cinquiesme Livre des Odes
Les Mascarades, combats et cartels
Le Bocage
Les Poemes
Traduction de quelques epigrammes grecz
Epitaphes de divers sujets

Note: The original Ronsard texts are reproduced from
the two-volume Bibliothèque de la Pléiade critical edition, *Œuvres
complètes* (Paris: Gallimard, 1993–1994), prepared by Jean Céard,
Daniel Ménager, and Michel Simonin, hereinafter cited
as Céard-Ménager-Simonin. [NRS]

LE PREMIER LIVRE DES
AMOURS

Qui voudra voir comme Amour me surmonte,
Comme il m'assaut, comme il se fait vainqueur,
Comme il r'enflame et r'englace mon cueur,
Comme il reçoit un honneur de ma honte:

Qui voudra voir une jeunesse pronte
À suivre en vain l'objet de son malheur,
Me vienne lire: il voirra la douleur,
Dont ma Deesse et mon Dieu ne font conte.

Il cognoistra qu' Amour est sans raison,
Un doux abus, une belle prison,
Un vain espoir qui de vent nous vient paistre:

Et cognoistra que l'homme se deçoit,
Quand plein d'erreur un aveugle il reçoit
Pour sa conduite, un enfant pour son maistre.

If one would see how Love has mastered me,
How he assails and conquers with his art,
How, now with fire, now ice, he plagues my heart,
How he seeks glory from my misery;

If one would see beau's yearning agony
For belle, who naught but torment will impart,
Read on: here will he see the sting, the smart,
That God and Goddess mine deal recklessly.★

Well will he learn that Love, unreasoning,
Is a sweet woe, a lovely prisoning,
A gust of wind that feeds our hope in vain:

Well will he learn that man is much beguiled—
Indeed, benighted—when he lets a child,
And one unsighted, as his master reign.

Le Premier Livre des Amours, I

(handwritten margin notes: Love takes on a powerful presence; Mimics The Petrarchan Sonnet — unrequited love — attracted to torment; —love takes on a character here also)*

★A previous variant of this line ("Dont ma Maistresse et Amour en font conte")—in a poem that knew many other variants throughout—makes clear that the "God and Goddess" in question are Cupid and the poet's mistress. (See Céard-Ménager-Simonin 1:1223–1224.) [NRS]

Puisse advenir qu'une fois je me vange
De ce penser qui devore mon cueur,
Et qui tousjours comme un lion veinqueur
Le tient, l'estrangle et sans pitié le mange!★

Avec le temps le temps mesme se change:
Mais ce cruel qui suçe ma vigueur,
Opiniastre à garder sa rigueur,
En autre lieu qu'en mon cœur ne se range.

Il est bien vray qu'il contraint un petit,
Durant le jour son secret appetit,
Et sur mon cœur ses griffes il n'allonge:

Mais quand le soir tient le jour enfermé,
Il sort en queste et lion affamé
De mille dents toute nuict il me ronge.

★The image of a lion that devours the lover's heart is a rewriting of the
Prometheus myth in which the god, strapped to a rock, has his liver gnawed
by a vulture. The eternally tortured Prometheus was a prominent figure in
love poetry. See Maurice Scève, *Délie*, LXXVII, ll. 3–5: "Ce grand désir de
mon bien oblyé / Dedans l'Enfer de ma mort immortelle, / Ronge l'esprit
par une fureur telle." Scève does not reveal the name of the victim until l. 10
of his *dizain;* Ronsard does not at all, but the allusion is clear in his final word
of the sonnet, "ronge," which appears consistently in the telling of the myth.
Compare *Amours* I, XXXV, with Ronsard's *Amours* I, XXXI, where the
myth of Prometheus earlier appeared, again masked by figures: "En lieu
d'un Aigle, un Soin cruellement / Souillant sa griffe en ma playe eternelle, /
Ronge mon cœur." (See Céard-Ménager-Simonin 1:31). [HG]

Oh, that I might, but once, in my distress,
Wreak vengeance on that thought that feeds on me;
That, like a conquering lion, ceaselessly
Clutches my heart, devours it, pitiless.

Time changes everything, they say; ah, yes,
But not this creature's cruel tenacity
That sucks my strength; for, evermore will he
Lurk in my heart to work his wickedness.

Indeed, by day, he can hold back his claw
And put to rest the cravings of his craw,
Rein in a bit his secret appetite:

But when day wanes, by evening penned, ah! then
Will he, the famished lion, quit his den,
A-quest, fangs bared, and gnaw me through the night.

Le Premier Livre des Amours, XXXV

De ses cheveux la rousoyante Aurore
Espars en l'air les Indes remplissoit,
Et ja le Ciel à longs traits rougissoit
De maint émail qui le matin decore,

Quand elle veit la Nymphe que j'adore,
Tresser son chef, dont l'or qui jaunissoit,
Le crespe honneur du sien esblouissoit,
Voire elle-mesme et tout le Ciel encore.

Lors ses cheveux vergongneuse arracha,
Et en pleurant sa face elle cacha,
Tant la beauté mortelle luy ennuie:★

Puis en poussant maint soupir en avant,
De ses soupirs fist enfanter un vent,
Sa honte un feu, et ses yeux une pluye.

★This Petrarchan conceit—the comparison of the poet's lady to the dawn, to the detriment of the latter—occurs often in Ronsard and his contemporaries, and would have a lengthy development culminating in the early seventeenth-century *précieux* (and typically French) literary quarrel surrounding sonnets composed on the theme of La Belle Matineuse (The Beautiful Morning-Damsel) by Vincent Voiture, Claude de Malleville, and others. [NRS]

Dawn, with her ruddy locks tousling throughout
The brightening East, was lightly coloring
The Skies, filling the air with reddening
Shafts of a pallid hue, around, about,

When, all at once, she saw my Nymph step out,
My heart's adored, whose tresses, glistening,
Dazzling, shone forth, surpassing everything:
Her hair, herself, and Heaven too, little doubt.

Then did Dawn, much abashed, tear out her hair,
And, weeping, hide her face in sad despair,
Such did mere mortal beauty cause her pain:

Whence, sobbing many a sigh, and sore chagrined,
Her sighs bore and brought forth a mighty wind;
Her shame spawned flame and fire; her eyes, the rain.

Le Premier Livre des Amours, XCV

Puis que je n'ay pour faire ma retraite
Du labyrinth, qui me va seduisant,
Comme Thesée, un filet conduisant
Mes pas douteux dans les erreurs de Crete:

Eussay-je au moins une poitrine faite
Ou de crystal, ou de verre luisant,
Ton œil iroit dedans mon cœur lisant
De quelle foy mon amour est parfaite.

Si tu sçavois de quelle affection
Je suis captif de ta perfection,
La mort seroit un confort à ma plainte:

Et lors peut estre esprise de pitié,
Tu pousserois sur ma despouille esteinte,
Quelque souspir de tardive amitié.

Since I no thread possess, like Theseus,
To guide my faltering steps out of the maze
Wherein he spent his Cretan nights and days,
Perplexed am I, a wanderer amorous.

Would that, at least, I had a luminous
Bosom, of crystal wrought; then could your gaze
See with what faith unblemished my heart pays
Homage to your perfection, ever thus.

Could you but know how deep my passion's thrall
To that perfection, then by death withal
Would my distress surely be comforted:

And then, perchance, less cold and pitiless,
Might you bestow upon my ashes spread—
Too late, alas!—a sigh of tenderness.

Le Premier Livre des Amours, CLXVIII

Baiser

Quand hors de tes lévres décloses,
(Comme entre deux fleuris sentiers)
Je sens ton haleine de roses,
Les miennes les avant-portiers
Du baiser, se rougissent d'aise,
Et de mes souhaits tous entiers
Me font jouyr, quand je te baise.★
Car l'humeur du baiser appaise,
S'escoulant au cœur peu à peu,
Ceste chaude amoureuse braise,
Dont tes yeux allumoient le feu.

★See p. 124, note. Ronsard is inspired in this poem by the Neo-Latin poet
Jean Second (Johannes Secundus), whose *Basia* created a vogue for kiss
poems that often seem to parody the Neoplatonic definition of love as
spiritus, or the exchange of breath between two lovers. The *Basia* reappeared
in Second's *Opera* (1541) and in later editions of the *Opera* (1561 and 1582),
and whereas Ronsard keeps here to the sensuality of the kiss, Jean Second
portrays violent kissing where tongues and lips are savagely bitten. Like
Marot, Ronsard and his fellow poets of the Pléiade wrote erotic poems that
circulated anonymously. [HG]

Kiss

When (as between two flowering lanes)
Your parted lips exhale the scent
Of roses that your breath contains,
Mine, at the kiss's sweet portent,
Flush with delight: my passions rise
And thrill my being, and I lie spent,
As, lips to lips, I kiss my prize.
For kiss's humors, in calm wise,
Flow to the heart, quell my desire:
The smouldering love that your bright eyes
Ignited to a flaming fire.

Le Premier Livre des Amours
(following Sonnet CCXXVII)

LE SECOND LIVRE DES AMOURS

Je vous envoie un bouquet que ma main
Vient de trier de ces fleurs épanies:
Qui ne les eût à ce vêpre cueillies,
Chutes à terre elles fussent demain.

Cela vous soit un exemple certain
Que vos beautés, bien qu'elles soient fleuries,
En peu de temps cherront toutes flétries,
Et comme fleurs périront tout soudain.

Le tems s'en va, le tems s'en va, ma Dame,
Las! Le tems, non, mais nous nous en allons,
Et tost serons estendus sous la lame:

Et des amours, desquelles nous parlons,
Quand serons morts, n'en sera plus nouvelles:
Pour-ce aimez moy, ce pendant qu'estes belle.

[handwritten annotations: nature is a part of the earthly world – making it not part of the The Neoplatonic ascent – making it follow line of carnal / physical desire]

I send you this bouquet, these flowers that I
Plucked with my own hands, blossoms blooming bright: *[seizing the present]*
Had no one chanced to pick them by this night,
Doubtless tomorrow would they fallen lie. *[almost past prime]*

Let them be an example: by and by, *[sexual in nature]*
Like them, your charms, though now they bloom aright,
Will see their petaled beauty fade from sight, *[moment is fleeting]*
To wither, fall, alas! and straightway die. *[physical beauty]*

Time flies, time flies, madame! Alas, time? No,
We it is, rather; we, who fly, who flee *[seems like an ascent]*
The earth above, soon to be laid below: *[only to be contradicted]*

And loves we prattle of will silenced be *[could be seen as spiritual – but ends w/ a physical desire]*
Once we lie dead, madame. Wherefore, beware!
Pray, love me now whilst yet you flourish fair. *[physical beauty w/ a physical desire]*

[handwritten: love in present moment]   *Le Second Livre des Amours,* [VI]*

*This sonnet, which exists in several variants, is one of forty-five poems
published in the *Œuvres* of 1572 and subsequently withdrawn. It is presented
in Céard-Ménager-Simonin under the rubric "Pièces présentes en 1572 au
'Second Livre des Amours' et retranchées en 1578" (Pléiade 1:270 and note,
p. 1332). The collection entitled *Le Second Livre des Amours,* first published in
1560, contains poems from earlier works published in the 1550s, including
the *Continuation des Amours* (1555) and *Nouvelle Continuation des Amours*
(1556), to which Ronsard added some pieces from the *Meslanges* (1559).
Anthologized on occasion as "Les Amours de Marie," the poems of the
Second Livre des Amours celebrate the provincial girl Marie d'Anjou. [HG]

Marie tout ainsi que vous m'avez tourné
Ma raison qui de libre est maintenant servile,
Ainsi m'avez tourné mon grave premier stile,
Qui pour chanter si bas n'estoit point ordonné.★

Au moins si vous m'aviez pour ma perte donné
Congé de manier vostre cuisse gentile,
Ou bien si vous estiez à mes desirs facile,
Je n'eusse regretté mon stile abandonné.

Las! ce qui plus me deult, c'est que n'estes contante
De voir que ma Muse est si basse et si rampante,
Qui souloit apporter aux François un effroy:

Mais vostre peu d'amour ma loyauté tourmente,
Et sans aucun espoir d'une meilleure attente
Tousjours vous me liez et triomphez de moy.

★See *Le Second Livre des Amours,* I, addressed to poet Pontus de Tyard, where Ronsard complains that the public that had originally complained of his hermeticism has condemned him for speaking too familiarly: "Tyard, on me blasmoit à mon commencement, / Dequoy j'estois obscur au simple populaire: / Mais on dit aujourd'huy que je suis au contraire, / Et que je me démens parlant trop bassement" (Céard-Ménager-Simonin 1:172). [HG]

Marie, just as you have transformed my sense,
Which, erstwhile free, is now become a slave,
So have you changed my art, once noble, grave,
Not made to sing in base subservience.

At least if you your leave had granted, whence
I might your thigh caress, or, randy knave,
Surfeit my lust with ease on all I crave,
I should not now lament past eloquence.

Alas! What grieves me is to see you so
Indifferent to my Muse, groveling low,
That once made Frenchmen stand in awe of me.

Loyal am I; and though your lack of love
Flouts and torments me with no hope thereof,
Yet still you bind me, flaunt your victory.

Le Second Livre des Amours, LX

Chanson

Je suis un demi-dieu quand assis vis-à-vis
De toy mon cher souci j'escoute les devis,
Devis entre-rompus d'un gracieux sou-rire,
Sou-ris qui me retient le cœur emprisonné:
En contemplant tes yeux je me pasme estonné,
Et de mes pauvres flancs un seul vent je ne tire.

Ma langue s'engourdist, un petit feu me court
Fretillant sous la peau: je suis muet et sourd,
Un voile sommeillant dessus mes yeux demeure:
Mon sang devient glacé, le courage me faut,
Mon esprit s'évapore, et alors peu s'en faut,
Que sans ame à tes pieds estendu je ne meure.★

★Rémy Belleau, a fellow Pléiade poet, published an edition of *Le Second Livre des Amours* in 1560, to which he added notes, glosses, and paraphrases of the poems. The effect was to show that Ronsard's "low style" was not without erudition. Following this chanson he writes: "This is a translation of the Ode of Sappho. . . . Reading it, you will admire it even if you have never been wounded by affection and passionate love, which are both depicted here." See Belleau, *Commentaire au Second Livre des Amours de Ronsard,* published by Marie Madeleine Fontaine and François Lecercle (Geneva: Droz, 1986), 82v. [HG]

Song

A demigod am I when, sitting there
Before you, face to face, O dear despair,
I listen to your banter, filled with awe,
Watching the smiles you smile the while: those eyes
That tyrannize my heart in wanton wise;
Nor from my bosom can I one breath draw.

Heavy, my tongue grows mute, and not a thing
I hear; beneath my skin goes flittering
A little flame; my eyes, veiled, lifeless lie:
Weak grows my heart, my blood runs cold as ice,
My mind dissolves, melts, and in but a trice
My soul could, at your feet, lie down and die.

death also
Common theme

Le Second Livre des Amours, Chanson
(preceding Sonnet LXI)

L'an se rajeunissoit en sa verde jouvence,
Quand je m'épris de vous, ma Sinope cruelle:★
Seize ans estoyent la fleur de vostre âge nouvelle,
Et vostre teint sentoit encore son enfance.

Vous aviez d'une infante encor la contenance,
La parolle, et les pas, vostre bouche estoit belle,
Vostre front, et voz mains dignes d'une immortelle,
Et vostre œil qui me fait trespasser quand j'y pense.

Amour, qui ce jour là si grandes beautez vit,
Dans un marbre, en mon cœur d'un trait les escrivit:
Et si pour le jourd'huy voz beautez si parfaites

Ne sont comme autresfois, je n'en suis moins ravy:
Car je n'ay pas égard à cela que vous estes,
Mais au dous souvenir des beautez que je vy.

★Originally one of sixteen love sonnets composed in honor of Sinope
(from the Greek, meaning "one who wounds the eyes") in *Le Second Livre des
Meslanges* (1559), this poem was later included in *Le Second Livre des Amours,*
but was subsequently removed. It is included in Céard-Ménager-Simonin
under the rubric "Pièces présentes en 1572 au 'Second Livre des Amours' et
retranchées en 1578." [NRS]

The year had, once again, turned young and green,
When I gave you my love, cruel Sinope;
Your eyes still shone with child's simplicity;
Still bloomed the flower of your years sixteen.

Still yours, youth's lively step, and speech, and mien;
Still beautiful your lips, a joy to see;
Comely hands, brow, like some divinity,
And hair that shamed the Sun incarnadine.

That day, Love spied your charms, and with his dart
Engraved them in the marble of my heart;
And if, this day, those beauties exquisite

Shine less than then, no less am I astir:
For what you are concerns me not a whit,
So sweet my memories now of what you were.

Le Second Livre des Amours, [LXI]

[handwritten margin note: Shifts between too ripe and not ripe enough]

Rossignol mon mignon, qui par cette saulaye★
Vas seul de branche en branche à ton gré voletant,
Et chantes à l'envy de moy qui vay chantant
Celle qui faut tousjours que dans la bouche j'aye,

Nous souspirons tous deux, ta douce voix s'essaye
De sonner les amours d'une qui t'ayme tant,
Et moy triste je vais la beauté regrettant
Qui m'a fait dans le cœur une si aigre playe.

Toutes-fois, Rossignol, nous differons d'un poinct,
C'est que tu es aymé, et je ne le suis point,
Bien que tous deux ayons les musiques pareilles:

Car tu fléchis t'amye au doux bruit de tes sons,
Mais la mienne qui prent à dépit mes chansons
Pour ne les escouter, se bouche les oreilles.

★See p. 284, note.

O Nightingale, my precious, who go flying,
Flitting among the willows, tree to tree,
Warbling my lady's scorn—ah, misery!—
That I, myself, am ever singing, sighing.

We sigh, we sing, we two: you, ever trying
To coo your lady's love to life; for me,
Sadly I sing the beauty that must be
Lost to my wounded heart, sick unto dying.

But, Nightingale, although we sigh and sing
A common song, we differ in one thing:
Much loved are you, but not I, not a jot.

For with the dulcet trillings of your art
You melt the chill within your lady's heart:
Mine, spurning, shuts her ears and hears mine not.

Le Second Livre des Amours, [XCI]

Comme on voit sur la branche au mois de May la rose★
En sa belle jeunesse, en sa premiere fleur,
Rendre le ciel jaloux de sa vive couleur,
Quand l'Aube de ses pleurs au poinct du jour l'arrose:

La grace dans sa fueille, et l'amour se repose,
Embasmant les jardins et les arbres d'odeur:
Mais batue ou de pluye, ou d'excessive ardeur,
Languissante elle meurt fueille à fueille déclose.

Ainsi en ta premiere et jeune nouveauté,
Quand la terre et le ciel honoroient ta beauté,
La Parque t'a tuee, et cendre tu reposes.

Pour obseques reçoy mes larmes et mes pleurs,
Ce vase plein de laict, ce panier plein de fleurs,
Afin que vif et mort ton corps ne soit que roses.

★This poem and the one following are from a cycle of thirteen on "La Mort de Marie" (The Death of Marie) that constitute the second part of *Le Second Livre des Amours*. Most, if not all, of these poems sing Ronsard's love, not of the idealized Marie d'Anjou, as is most often thought, but of Marie de Clèves, wife of Henri de Bourbon, prince de Condé. See the Céard-Ménager-Simonin edition, where the editors note the influence on Ronsard of Petrarch's poems on the death of Laura. Therein Ronsard found a theme that unified the second part of his own *Second Livre des Amours* and concealed its intended subjects: Marie de Clèves and the grieving Henri III. There are numerous echoes of Petrarch in this sequence. [HG]

[handwritten: on the earth]

Just as, upon the branch, one sees the rose's
Bud bloom in May, young blossom newly spread
Before the sky, jealous of its bright red,
As Dawn, sprinkling her tears, the morn discloses: *[handwritten: earthly]*

Beauty lies in its leaf, and love reposes, *[handwritten: lies dead]*
Wafting its scent on tree, bush, flowerbed:
But, lashed by rain or torrid heat, soon dead, *[handwritten: of some sort]*
Leaf after leaf its fragile grace exposes. *[handwritten: violation of some sort]*

So too, blooming with youth, as earth and heaven *[handwritten: equating earth & heaven]*
Honored your beauty, to Fate was it given
To slay your flesh, which now in ash reposes. *[handwritten: harsh — also does not seem spiritual]*
[handwritten: violent!]
Take thus these tears that I, in tribute, shed,
This jug of milk, these blossoms heaped, outspread,
So that in death, as life, that flesh be roses.★ *[handwritten: lies dead]*

Le Second Livre des Amours, II, IV

[handwritten: does not seem spiritual — no discussion of ascent]

[handwritten: spec. in terms of flesh]

[handwritten: really subverts Neoplatonic ascent — life & death the same — no ascent — purely carnal]

[handwritten: beauty passing can be used as an argument of the vanity of human existence — but it can also be telling of a physical desire, as Ronsard wants this woman when she is young & beautiful]

★Given Ronsard's intentional (and uncharacteristic) repetition of whole words at the rhyme, I have taken the liberty of ignoring one of the strictures of traditional English prosody against that practice, to reproduce his effect. [NRS]

Quand je pense à ce jour, où je la vey si belle
Toute flamber d'amour, d'honneur et de vertu,
Le regret, comme un traict mortellement pointu,
Me traverse le cœur d'une playe eternelle.

Alors que j'esperois la bonne grace d'elle,
Amour a mon espoir par la mort combatu:
La mort a son beau corps d'un cercueil revestu,
Dont j'esperois la paix de ma longue querelle.

Amour, tu es enfant inconstant et leger:
Monde, tu es trompeur pipeur et mensonger,
Decevant d'un chacun l'attente et le courage.

Malheureux qui se fie en l'amour et en toy:
Tous deus comme la mer vous n'avez point de foy
La mer tousjours parjure, Amour tousjours volage.

When I think of that day, when she appeared
In all her beauty, virtuous, glorious,
Aflame with love, woe's dart perfidious
Pierces my heart, with sorrow ever seared. *amazing!*

Just as I mused that she whom I revered
Would grant my hope, Love slew it, traitorous:
The coffin clothes her beauty now; and, thus,
Fled both my dream and the rebuke I feared.

Love, you are much the most capricious child;
Life, you deceive us, by your lies beguiled,
Dashing our hopes, sating our passions never.

Unhappy he who trusts in love and you:
Both, like the sea, you waver, false, untrue—
O treacherous sea, O Love, inconstant ever!

Le Second Livre des Amours, II, VII

SONNETS ET MADRIGALS POUR ASTREE

À mon retour (hé! je m'en desespere)
Tu m'as receu d'un baiser tout glacé,
Froid, sans saveur, baiser d'un trespassé,
Tel que Diane en donnoit à son frere,

Tel qu'une fille en donne à sa grand'mere,
La fiancée en donne au fiancé,
Ny savoureux ny moiteux ny pressé:
Et quoy, ma lévre est-elle si amere?

Hà, tu devrois imiter les pigeons
Qui bec en bec de baisers doux et longs
Se font l'amour sur le haut d'une souche.

Je te suppli' maistresse desormais
Ou baise moy la saveur en la bouche,
Ou bien du tout ne me baise jamais.★

★As previously noted, the kiss poems are inspired by the *Basia* of Johannes Secundus, a Neo-Latin Dutch humanist. (See notes, pp. 124 and 276.) Several of the Pléiade poets composed *baisers*, but the view that poets should be writing in Latin was not acceptable to some humanists, among them Jacques Peletier. The latter wrote in his *Art poétique* (1555): "Quelle sorte de nation sommes-nous, de parler éternellement par la bouche d'autrui?" (Quoted in Warner Forrest Patterson, *Three Centuries of French Poetic Theory* [Ann Arbor: University of Michigan Press, 1935], p. 449.) [HG]

On my return (ah! what dismay I faced),
Cold was the kiss you gave me, tasteless; nay,
Worse still: a corpse's kiss; a kiss, the way
Diana kissed her brother, scarce embraced;★

Like a granddaughter's kiss, or like the chaste
Kiss a betrothed gives to her fiancé;
Not moist, or passion-pressed, or savory, they:
What? Are my lips so bitter to your taste?

Ah! Rather like two pigeons let us be,
Who, beak to beak, kiss endlessly, and who
Make sweet and tender love atop their tree.

Henceforth, I beg you, if you kiss me ever,
Let savory be those lips, my love, that you
Press against mine; else, best you kiss me never.

Sonnets et madrigals pour Astree, XIV

★Céard-Ménager-Simonin (1:1354) calls attention to the Ovidian origin
of this reference: *Metamorphoses* 1.5.452ff. [NRS]

LE PREMIER LIVRE DES
SONNETS POUR HÉLÈNE

Ce premier jour de May, Helene, je vous jure
Par Castor par Pollux, vos deus freres jumeaux,
Par la vigne enlassee à l'entour des ormeaux,
Par les prez par les bois herissez de verdure,

Par le nouveau Printemps fils aisné de Nature,
Par le cristal qui roule au giron des ruisseaux,
Par tous les rossignols, miracle des oiseaux,
Que seule vous serez ma derniere aventure.

Vous seule me plaisez, j'ay par election★
Et non à la volée aimé vostre jeunesse:
Aussi je prens en gré toute ma passion,

Je suis de ma fortune autheur, je le confesse:
La vertu m'a conduit en telle affection.
Si la vertu me trompe adieu belle Maistresse.

★The phrase "par election" emphasizes the poet's claim that he is not a victim of fate. *Election* derives from the Latin *electio* (choice). [HG]

Hélène, on May's first day, here I declare,
By your twin brothers, heaven's Gemini,
By meads, by vines and elms entwined thereby,
By woods that now their bristling verdure wear,

By Springtime, Nature's eldest son and heir,
By crystal-bosomed brooklets flowing high,
By nightingales, winged miracles, do I
Vow you are my last love: and this I swear.

None pleases me but you, and I adore
Your youth by choice, not whim, fair demoiselle;
My passion revels in its conqueror:

Mine alone is the blame, though, truth to tell,
Virtue it was who bade me love; wherefore,
If she deceives me, Mistress mine, farewell.

Le Premier Livre des Sonnets pour Hélène, I

Quoy? me donner congé de servir toute femme,
Et mon ardeur esteindre au premier corps venu,
Ainsi qu'un vagabond sans estre retenu,
Abandonner la bride au vouloir de ma flame:

Non, ce n'est pas aimer. L'Archer ne vous entame
Qu'un peut le haut du cœur d'un traict foible et menu.
Si d'un coup bien profond il vous estoit cognu,
Ce ne seroit que soulfre et braise de vostre ame.

En soupçon de vostre ombre en tous lieux vous seriez:
À toute heure en tous temps jalouse me suivriez,
D'ardeur et de fureur et de crainte allumee.

Amour au petit pas non au gallop vous court,
Et vostre amitié n'est qu'une flame de Court,
Où peu de feu se trouve et beaucoup de fumee.

What? You would give me leave to try my hand
With every woman, and, like vile outcast,
Quench my flame on the first that happens past,
And loose my love, unbridled, through the land?

Such is not love! The Archer, though he planned
To pierce you with his dart and hold you fast,
Alas, but grazed you: were your love to last,
Your brimstone soul would burn like flaming brand.

Jealous, you would pursue me roundabout,
Distrusting your own shadow, in and out,
Aflame with fear, and fury, and desire.

No! Love goes not a-gallop but a-crawl
In you: yours is a Court-bred flame withal,
With smoke a-plenty but with little fire.

Le Premier Livre des Sonnets pour Hélène, XX

LE SECOND LIVRE DES
SONNETS POUR HÉLÈNE

Trois jours sont ja passez que je suis affamé
De vostre doux regard, et qu'à l'enfant je semble
Que sa nourrice laisse, et qui crie et qui tremble
De faim en son berceau, dont il est consommé.

Puis que mon œil ne voit le vostre tant aimé,
Qui ma vie et ma mort en un regard assemble,
Vous deviez, pour le moins, m'escrire, ce me semble:
Mais vous avez le cœur d'un rocher enfermé.

Fiere ingrate beauté trop hautement superbe,
Vostre courage dur n'a pitié de l'amour,
Ny de mon palle teint ja flestry comme une herbe.

Si je suis sans vous voir deux heures à sejour,
Par espreuve je sens ce qu'on dit en proverbe,
L'amoureux qui attend se vieillist en un jour.★

★Not exactly proverbial, even in Ronsard's time, the allusion is explained in Céard-Ménager-Simonin 1:1382 as referring to a line in Theocritus (*Idylls* 12.5.2). [NRS]

Three days have I not seen your face, and I
Hunger for your sweet glance; I feel as though
I were a trembling, mewling babe, with no
Nursemaid to feed him, till he starve and die.

Since I may not behold you, eye to eye,
Whose glance decrees if I must die or go
On living, might you write at least! But oh,
Your stone-clad heart cares neither how nor why.

Proud beauty, whose cruel breast no tender ruth
Feels for my woe; nor for my hue, grown gray,
Pallid, like withered grass, fled now my youth:

Two hours without you spent, and such dismay
Know I, that I lament the proverb's truth:
"Waiting turns lover old in but one day."

Le Second Livre des Sonnets pour Hélène, XI

Quand vous serez bien vieille, au soir à la chandelle,
Assise aupres du feu, devidant et filant,
Direz chantant mes vers, en vous esmerveillant,
Ronsard me celebroit du temps que j'estois belle.

Lors vous n'aurez servante oyant telle nouvelle,
Desja sous le labeur à demy sommeillant,
Qui au bruit de mon nom ne s'aille resveillant,
Benissant vostre nom de louange immortelle.

Je seray sous la terre et fantôme sans os
Par les ombres myrteux je prendray mon repos:
Vous serez au fouyer une vieille accroupie,

Regrettant mon amour et vostre fier desdain.
Vivez, si m'en croyez, n'attendez à demain:
Cueillez dés aujourdhuy les roses de la vie.

When you are very old, by candle's flame,
Spinning beside the fire, at end of day,
Singing my verse, admiring, you will say:
"When I was fair, Ronsard's muse I became."

Your servant then, some weary old beldame—
Whoever she may be—nodding away,
Hearing "Ronsard," will shake off sleep, and pray
Your name be blessed, to live in deathless fame.

Buried, I shall a fleshless phantom be,
Hovering by the shadowed myrtle tree;
You, by the hearth, a pining crone, bent low,

Whose pride once scorned my love, much to your sorrow.
Heed me, live for today, wait not the morrow:
Gather life's roses while still fresh they grow.

Le Second Livre des Sonnets pour Hélène, XLIII

[handwritten annotations:]
concerned w/ his own claim to fame
Du Bellay & Ronsard life their names in their poetry
time seize moment
blooming (again)
describes old age in a very carnal way
—again subverting ascent to "true" beauty

LES AMOURS DIVERSES

Je voudrois bien n'avoir jamais tasté
Si follement le tetin de m'amie:
Sans ce malheur l'autre plus grande envie
Ne m'eust jamais le courage tenté.

Comme un poisson pour s'estre trop hasté,
Par un appast suit la fin de sa vie:
Ainsi je vais où la mort me convie,
D'un beau tetin doucement appasté.

Qui eust pensé que le cruel destin
Eust enfermé sous un si beau tetin
Un si grand feu pour m'en faire la proye?

Advisez donc quel seroit le coucher,
Quand le peché d'un seul petit toucher
Ne me pardonne, et les mains me foudroye?

Oh, how I wish that I had never laid
My foolish hand upon my damsel's breast!
I should not now be hopelessly obsessed
To press my passion further with the maid.

But, like a fish, alas! I shall have paid
My very life as price for my unrest:
A nipple was my lure; I am possessed,
And surely death will end my escapade.

Who could have thought that unkind fate would place
Within a nipple of such beauteous grace
A fire so hot that it would martyr me?

If I must suffer, for one harmless touch,
A thousand deaths, imagine then how much
More deadly lying in her arms would be.

Les Amours diverses, Sonnet IX

Ô de repos et d'amour toute pleine
Chambrette heureuse, où deux heureux flambeaux
De deux beaux yeux plus que les Astres beaux,
Me font escorte apres si longue peine!

Or' je pardonne à la mer inhumaine,
Aux flots, aux vents, mon naufrage et mes maux,
Puis que par tant et par tant de travaux
Une main douce à si doux port me meine.

Adieu tormente, adieu tempeste, adieu
Vous flots cruels, ayeux du petit Dieu,★
Qui dans mon sang a sa fleche souillée:

Ores encré dedans le sein du port,
En vœu promis j'appan dessus le bord
Aux Dieux marins ma despouille mouillée.†

★As son of Venus, herself born of the waters, Cupid was their grandson.
[NRS]
†According to ancient tradition, as cited in Horace (*Odes* 1.5.13–16),
sailors saved from shipwreck would hang their clothes on the shore in tribute
to the gods of the sea. (See Céard-Ménager-Simonin 1:1410.) [NRS]

her body?

O happy little chamber, where repose
And love reside; where gladsome torches twain
Glow by my side, now finished my long pain:
Two eyes like Stars, but fairer still than those!

I pardon now the sea's fell ebbs and flows,
Though tempest-tossed, shipwrecked again, again,
Since now a soft and gentle hand would fain
Lead me to such a port and end my woes.

Adieu foul winds; adieu storms, squalls; adieu
To you, cruel waves, forebears of Cupid, who,
Child God, has steeped his arrow in my blood.

Now anchored, nestled safe in port, I keep   *sexually charged*
My vow, and unto you, Gods of the deep,   *— he has finally*
I hang my dripping garments by the flood.   *got her*

Les Amours diverses, XI

Petit nombril, que mon penser adore,★
Et non mon œil qui n'eut oncques le bien
De te voir nud, et qui merites bien
Que quelque ville on te bastisse encore.

Signe amoureux, duquel Amour s'honore,
Representant l'Androgyne lien,
Et le courroux du grand Saturnien,
Dont le nombril tousjours se rememore.†

Ny ce beau chef ny ces yeux ny ce front,
Ny ce beau sein où les fleches se font,
Que les beautez diversement se forgent,

Ne me pourroyent ma douleur conforter,
Sans esperer quelque jour de taster
Ton compagnon où les amours se logent.

★On the popularity of the *blason* poems celebrating various parts of the
female body, see pp. 98–99.
†Céard-Ménager-Simonin 1:1410 cites Robert V. Merrill's article "The
Pléiade and the Androgyne," *Comparative Literature* (1949), 97–112, discussing
this and other allusions to Jupiter's wrathful division of primitive man
into two separate beings, male and female. [NRS]

O little navel, who my thoughts inflame,
And not my eyes—for never have I had
The privilege of seeing you unclad,
You, who deserve a city in your name;

Symbol of Love and sign of his acclaim,
Remnant of Jove's wild rage, who, near gone mad,
Severed the Androgyne we were, then bade
Us mindful be that we, thus, two became:

Neither that brow, that comely head, those eyes,
Nor that fair bosom where two darts arise,
Nor all those beauties formed, below, above,

Could soothe my pain or comfort me, unless
Hope had I that, one day, I might caress
That tender mate of yours, the seat of love.

Les Amours diverses, XII

Petite Nymphe folâtre,
Nymphette que j'idolâtre,
Ma mignonne, dont les yeux
Logent mon pis et mon mieux:
Ma doucette, ma sucrée,
Ma Grace, ma Cytherée,
Tu me dois pour m'appaiser
Mille fois le jour baiser.
Tu m'en dois au matin trente,
Puis apres disner cinquante,
Et puis vingt apres souper.
Et quoy? me veux-tu tromper?

Avance mes quartiers, belle,
Ma tourtre, ma colombelle:
Avance-moy les quartiers
De mes paymens tous entiers.

Demeure, où fuis-tu Maistresse?
Le desir qui trop me presse,
Ne sçauroit arrester tant,
S'il n'est payé tout contant.

Revien revien mignonnette,
Mon doux miel, ma violette,
Mon œil, mon cœur, mes amours,
Ma cruelle, qui tousjours
Trouves quelque mignardise,
Qui d'une douce feintise
Peu à peu mes forces fond,
Comme on voit dessus un mont
S'escouler la neige blanche:
Ou comme la rose franche

O little Nymph, who frolic free,
Who make a worshiper of me;
You, whose two eyes, my fair Nymphet,
All of my best and worst beget:
My Grace, my Venus; who, I pray,
A thousand kisses, every day,
Upon me, to dispel my woe
And ease my anguish, ought bestow:
Thirty at morningtide, and then
Another fifty kisses when
Dinner is finished; and still more
When suppertime is done: a score.
Or, do you think that numbers such
Of kisses are, for me, too much?

Come, pay me what you owe, my love,
My pigeon-pet, my turtledove:
Come, Mistress mine, and pay your debt.

What? Would you fly and flee me yet?
Take care: the passion in my breast,
That spurs me on, will know no rest
Until the debt is fully paid.

Come back, come back, my flower-maid,★
My violet coy, my honey sweet,
My eye, my heart; come, *ma petite,*
You who are all my love, cruel thing,
Who, with your bluff and blandishing,
Sap all my force, my very strength:
Like mountain snows that melt, at length,
In flows of white; or like the rose

★My translation takes into account the wordplay of the original, in which
"mignonnette," meaning a "sweet little thing," is also the name of a flower, a
type of clover. [NRS]

Perd le vermeil de son teint
Des rais du Soleil esteint.

   Où fuis-tu mon Angelette,
Ma vie, mon amelette?
Appaise un peu ton courroux,
Assy-toy sur mes genoux,
Et de cent baisers appaise
De mon cœur la chaude braise.

   Donne moy bec contre bec,
Or' un moite, ores un sec,
Or' un babillard, et ores
Un qui soit plus long encores
Que ceux des pigeons mignars,
Couple à couple fretillars.

   Hà Dieu! ma douce Guerriere,
Tire un peu ta bouche arriere:
Le dernier baiser donné
A tellement estonné
De mille douceurs ma vie,
Que du sein me l'a ravie,
Et m'a fait voir à demi
Le Nautonnier ennemy,
Et les plaines où Catulle,
Et les rives où Tibulle,
Pas à pas se promenant,
Vont encore maintenant
De leurs bouchettes blesmies
Rebaisotans leurs amies.

That soon, beneath the Sun's rays, grows
Withered and pale, now red no more
The ruddy hue that once it wore.

　Whither flee you, O Angelkins?
Come, calm my burning heart's chagrins,
O you, my soul! Come, sit upon
My lap and let your wrath be gone;
And with a hundred kisses ease
The ardor of my agonies.

　Clasped beak to beak, like pigeons, let
One kiss be dry, and one be wet;
One, all a-babble and a-sputter;
One, longer yet, like birds a-flutter.

　Ah, God! My Warrior belle, avast!
Draw back your lips a bit: that last
Kiss, with such rapture sweetly given,
Near sent my ravished soul to heaven:
Indeed, it sucked my very breath
And left me almost kissed to death,
With visions of the Boatman fell,
And of Catullus' fields as well,
And of Tibullus' banks,* where they
Still stroll their loving hours away,
As, lips grown pale and wan, their shades
Peck at the shadows of fair maids.

Les Amours diverses, Chanson I

*The Boatman referred to is, of course, the mythological Charon, who transported the dead across the River Styx in the netherworld. The evocation of Latin lyric poets Catullus and Tibullus is a reference to their love-and-nature poetry, which, for the Classics-steeped Ronsard, obviously transcended death. [NRS]

GAYETEZ

Vœu d'un Pescheur aux Naiades★

Si de ma tremblante gaule
Je puis lever hors de l'eau
Pris à l'haim le gros barbeau
Qui hante au pied de ce saule,

Naiades des eaux profondes,
À vous je promets en vœu
De jamais n'estre reveu
Repescher desur vos ondes.
Et pour enseigne eternelle,
À ces saules verdelets
Je vous pendray mes filets,
Mes lignes et ma nacelle.

★Regarding the genre of the ex-voto, see pp. 234ff.

A Fisherman's Vow to the Naiads

If my fishing line, a-quiver,
Pulls that big fish that I see
Over by the willow tree—
That fat mullet—from the river,

Naiads of the waters deep,
Never shall I come again
Here to poach on your domain:
Lest this vow I fail to keep,
From those willow branches vernal
I shall hang, to honor you,
Lines, and nets, my basket too,
Symbols of my oath eternal.

Gayetez

Si nourrir grand' barbe au menton
Nous fait Philosophes paroistre,
Un bouc barbasse pourroit estre
Par ce moyen quelque Platon.*

---

*This quatrain, adapted from Palladas, and the one following, adapted
from Loukillios (see p. 374, note), are among eleven pieces originally pub-
lished with Ronsard's other Greek-inspired epigrams. They were eventually
assigned by him to the collection *Gayetez* in the 1584 edition of his *Œuvres*
under the rubric "Traduction de quelques autres epigrammes grecs," after a
variety of other placements. (See Céard-Ménager-Simonin 1:1456–1459.)
[NRS]

If a well-whiskered chin can duly
Make one appear the *philosophe,*
An old he-goat has beard enough
To make him seem a Plato, truly.

  Gayetez (*Traduction de quelques
  autres epigrammes grecs,* IV)

Si tu es viste à souper,
Et à courir mal-adestre,
Des pieds il te faut repaistre,
Et des lévres galoper.

If in a trice your mouth sups, sips,
But slow your gait, then it is meet
That you dine, rather, with your feet,
And gallop, rather, with your lips.

> *Gayetez* (*Traduction de quelques*
> *autres epigrammes grecs,* XI)

LIVRET DE FOLASTRIES

De Nicarche
Πορδὴ ἀποκτείνει πολλούς⋆

Le pet qui ne peut sortir
À maintz la mort fait sentir,
Et le pet de son chant donne
La vie à mainte personne.
Si donc un pet est si fort
Qu'il sauve, ou donne la mort,
D'un pet la force est egale
À la puissance royale.

⋆The Greek phrase, meaning "The fart repels many," is the opening line
of one of the brief pieces in the Palatine manuscript of the *Greek Anthology*
(XI, cccxcv), which, in addition to the original of Ronsard's translation,
contains another three dozen epigrams attributed to the first-century sa-
tiric poet Nikarchos, some perhaps falsely. (See Friedrich Jacobs, *Anthologie
grecque*, vol. 2 [Paris: Hachette, 1863], p. 389.) Céard-Ménager-Simonin
(1:1467) also calls attention to this poem's similarity to a passage in *The
Clouds* of Aristophanes (5.390ff.). [NRS]

The fart that holds its fetid breath,
Unspent, for many smacks of death;
The fart, unpent, that croons its air
Often foils death, dispels despair.
If, then, the fart is good or ill,
And if it can both spare and kill,
Thus does the fulsome fart, at length,
Equal the king in power and strength.

Livret de folastries, XIII, *De Nicarche*

Sonet

Lance au bout d'or qui sais et poindre et oindre,
De qui jamais la roideur ne defaut,
Quand en camp clos bras à bras il me faut
Toutes les nuis au dous combat me joindre.

Lance vraiment qui ne fus jamais moindre
À ton dernier qu'à ton premier assaut,
De qui le bout bravement dressé haut
Est toujours prest de choquer et de poindre.

Sans toi le Monde un Chaos se feroit,
Nature manque inabille seroit
Sans tes combas d'acomplir ses offices:

Donq, si tu es l'instrument de bon heur
Par qui l'on vit, combien à ton honneur
Doit on de vœus, combien de sacrifices?

O gold-tipped spear, you who both stick and prick:
Who, strong and straight and stout, ever anoint
My combats hand-to-hand, nor disappoint
In all my nightly dueling chivalric.

Proud, tireless minion mine, forever quick
To rise to duty, never out of joint,
Tip high, unbowed, thrusting a counterpoint
Against all victims, staunch through thin and thick.

The World without you would be nothingness,
Chaos; for Nature would be powerless
To undertake her sacred obligations.

To honor you, who prick and spur me on,*
How many a glory shall be yours anon:
Oaths, sacrifices, prayers, vows, incantations?

Livret de folastries, Sonet

---

*As indicated in the notes of Céard-Ménager-Simonin (1:1467–1468),
the original here, among other obvious *gauloiseries,* contains a spoonerism,
what in French is called a *contrepet* (or *contrepèterie*), which my translation can
only hint at, phonetically as well as lexically. [NRS]

L.M.F.★

Je te salue ô vermeillette fante,
Qui vivement entre ces flancs reluis:
Je te salue ô bienheuré pertuis,
Qui rens ma vie heureusement contante.

C'est toi qui fais que plus ne me tourmante
L'archer volant, qui causoit mes ennuis.
T'aiant tenu seulement quatre nuis,
Je sen sa force en moi desjà plus lente.

Ô petit trou, trou mignard, trou velu,
D'un poil folet mollement crespelu,
Qui à ton gré domtes les plus rebelles,

Tous vers galans devoient pour t'honorer
À beaus genous te venir adorer,
Tenans au poin leurs flambantes chandelles.

★Céard-Ménager-Simonin (1:1468) explains the enigmatic initials entit-
ling this poem, a sequel to the previous one, as standing for *le mesme féminin;*
that is, "the same [as the preceding, but] feminine." [NRS]

Good-day to you, O tender-crimsoned slit,
Who there, betwixt those flanks, sit glistening:
Good-day to you, fair-omened opening,
Who rule my life yet make a joy of it.

Because of you, that wingèd hypocrite,
Young Cupid, source of all my suffering,
Stings me no more: four nights with you, sweet thing,
And less feel I his power; nay, scarce a whit.

O little hole; hole cunning; hole bedecked
With tousled curls and swirls that can subject
The most rebellious to your lips' commands:

Let all our gallant swains come worship you,
Fall on their knees, and offer you your due,
Clutching their flaming candles in their hands.

Livret de folastries, L.M.F.

LE PREMIER LIVRE DES ODES

A sa maistresse*

Mignonne, allons voir si la rose
Qui ce matin avoit desclose
Sa robe de pourpre au Soleil,
A point perdu ceste vesprée
Les plis de sa robe pourprée,
Et son teint au vostre pareil.

Las! voyez comme en peu d'espace,
Mignonne, elle a dessus la place
Las las ses beautez laissé cheoir!
Ô vrayment marastre Nature,
Puis qu'une telle fleur ne dure
Que du matin jusques au soir!

Donc, si vous me croyez mignonne,
Tandis que vostre âge fleuronne
En sa plus verte nouveauté,
Cueillez cueillez vostre jeunesse:
Comme à ceste fleur la vieillesse
Fera ternir vostre beauté.

   *Also frequently entitled "Ode à Cassandre," this well-known poem was originally published in the 1553 edition of the *Amours* before being included, in 1555, in the first four books of Ronsard's *Odes*. (See Céard-Ménager-Simonin 1:1512.) [NRS]

To His Mistress

My pet, come see, this eventide,
If that fair rose that opened wide
Its crimson robe, at dawn, unto
The sun, sees not already flown
Its crimsoned folds, and, like your own,
Its blush of morning's tender hue.

Ah me, my pet! Alas, see what
A little time will do! In but
A trice, its beauty wilts, undone.
Stepmother nature! Wicked, she,
If such a flower—ah me! ah me!—
Lasts but from morn to setting sun.

Thus, if you heed my word, my pet,
Whilst childhood blooms and blossoms yet,
Green, fresh, and new, now is the hour:
Before it fades, pluck, pluck your youth,
Lest, all too soon, old age, forsooth,
Wither your beauty, like the flower.

Le Premier Livre des Odes, XVII

LE SECOND LIVRE DES ODES

Ode

Fay refraischir mon vin de sorte
Qu'il passe en froideur un glaçon:
Fay venir Janne, qu'elle apporte
Son luth pour dire une chanson:
Nous ballerons tous trois au son:
Et dy à Barbe qu'elle vienne
Les cheveux tors à la façon
D'une follastre Italienne.

Ne vois-tu que le jour se passe?
Je ne vy point au lendemain:
Page, reverse dans ma tasse,
Que ce grand verre soit tout plain.
Maudit soit qui languit en vain:
Ces vieux Medecins je n'appreuve:
Mon cerveau n'est jamais bien sain,
Si beaucoup de vin ne l'abreuve.

Ode

Come here and chill my wine, my friend;
For colder would I have it be
Than ice. Then straightway go and send
For damsel Jeanne, and tell her she
Should bring her lute; then shall we three
Dance to her tune; and have Barbe come
As well, braids twisted fetchingly,
Like lass Italian, frolicsome.

Can you not see how fast today
Dies with tomorrow, and flies on?
Page, come and fill my goblet, pray,
Full to the brim! A curse upon
Those who but languish—now, anon—
In vain; and graybeard Doctors too!
My brain grows weak; my spirit, wan,
Without my wine, gone all askew.

Le Second Livre des Odes, X

Odelette

Nature fist present de cornes aux toreaux,
De la crampe du pied pour armes aux chevaux,
Aux poissons le nouer, et aux aigles l'adresse
De trancher l'air soudain, aux liévres la vistesse,
Aux serpens le venin enveloppé dedans
Leur queue et leur gencive, et aux lions les dens,
À l'homme la prudence: et n'ayant plus puissance
De donner comme à l'homme, aux femmes la prudence,
Leur donna la beauté, pour les servir en lieu
De pistoles, de dars, de lances et d'espieu:
Car la beauté, Nicot, d'une plaisante dame
Surmonte hommes et Dieux, les armes et la flame.

Odelet

Nature gave horns to bulls for their defense;
To horses, hooves; to fish, preeminence
Of tail and fin; to eagles, skill of wing
To rend the air; to hares, their scampering;
To snakes, their venom, fore and aft; sharp teeth
To lions; whilst to man did she bequeath
His wisdom. But to women, inasmuch
As she was powerless to give them such,
Beauty, instead, she granted, to replace
The force of harquebus, and dart, and mace:
Sooner the Gods and men, Nicot, will be
Subdued by beauty than by weaponry.

Le Second Livre des Odes, XXVIII

LE QUATRIESME LIVRE DES

ODES

Ode

Quand je suis vingt ou trente mois
Sans retourner en Vandomois,
Plein de pensées vagabondes,
Plein d'un remors et d'un souci,
Aux rochers je me plains ainsi,
Aux bois, aux antres, et aux ondes.

Rochers, bien que soyez âgez
De trois mil ans, vous ne changez
Jamais ny d'estat ny de forme:
Mais tousjours ma jeunesse fuit,
Et la vieillesse qui me suit,
De jeune en vieillard me transforme.

Bois, bien que perdiez tous les ans
En l'hyver voz cheveux plaisans,
L'an d'apres qui se renouvelle,
Renouvelle aussi vostre chef:
Mais le mien ne peut de rechef
R'avoir sa perruque nouvelle.

Ode

When, for two years or three, I quit
Vendôme, and not return to it,
My thoughts go fleeting, dolorous;
Heartsore and filled with care, I go
Bewailing to the rocks my woe—
The woodlands, caverns, waters—thus:

"Rocks, who three thousand years have stood
Unchanged in shape and size! Ah, would
That I could likewise be! But see
How youth goes fleeing, flitting past;
How age, approaching all too fast,
Will soon make an old man of me.

"Woodlands, each year your comely tresses
Fall to the winter's chill caresses;
Still, when the spring the earth renews,
Your head it covers, full once more;
But mine no springtime can restore:
Now gone for good what once I lose.

Antres, je me suis veu chez vous
Avoir jadis verds les genous,
Le corps habile, et la main bonne:
Mais ores j'ay le corps plus dur,
Et les genous, que n'est le mur
Qui froidement vous environne.

Ondes, sans fin vous promenez
Et vous menez et ramenez
Vos flots d'un cours qui ne sejourne:
Et moy sans faire long sejour
Je m'en vais de nuict et de jour,
Au lieu d'où plus on ne retourne.

Si est-ce que je ne voudrois
Avoir esté rocher ou bois,
Pour avoir la peau plus espesse,
Et veincre le temps emplumé:
Car ainsi dur je n'eusse aimé
Toy qui m'as fait vieillir, Maistresse.

"Caverns, when I frequented you,
Doing the things that youth can do,
Limber was I of knee and hand;
Now stiff my limbs, and hard as stone,
Cold as your walls, my body grown,
Old and unfit, undone, unmanned.

"Waters, down to the sea descending,
Your waves come, go, in never-ending
Flow, never stopping, ever churning:
But I, by day, by night, move on
And on, to reach that place, anon,
Whence, lastly, there is no returning."

Yet, would I not a rock become,
Or woods, for all my martyrdom.
Thick-skinned might I have been, and bold
Enough to halt time's flight; but never
Could I have loved you howsoever,
Madame: you who have turned me old.

Le Quatriesme Livre des Odes, X

Ode

Ma douce jouvance est passée,
Ma premiere force est cassée,
J'ay la dent noire et le chef blanc,
Mes nerfs sont dissous, et mes veines,
Tant j'ay le corps froid, ne sont pleines
Que d'une eau rousse en lieu de sang.

Adieu ma lyre, adieu fillettes
Jadis mes douces amourettes,
Adieu, je sens venir ma fin:
Nul passetemps de ma jeunesse
Ne m'accompagne en la vieillesse,
Que le feu, le lict et le vin.

J'ay la teste tout eslourdie
De trop d'ans et de maladie,
De tous costez le soin me mord:
Et soit que j'aille ou que je tarde,
Tousjours apres moy je regarde
Si je verray venir la Mort:

Qui doit, ce me semble, à toute heure
Me mener là bas où demeure
Je ne sçay quel Pluton, qui tient
Ouvert à tous venans un antre,
Où bien facilement on entre,
Mais d'où jamais on ne revient.

Ode

Gone is my strength, sweet youth is fled,
My teeth are black, and white my head;
Sickly, my nerves are weaker growing;
So cold am I that in my veins
No blood of ruddy hue remains:
Naught but a reddish liquid flowing.

Farewell my lyre, farewell my belles,
You, once my tender damosels;
Farewell, I sense my days' decline:
Old age, alas, has borne away
The pastimes of a younger day,
Leaving but hearth, and bed, and wine.

Head bowed with ills and many a year—
Indeed, too many of both, I fear—
I feel the biting agony
Of care—here, there, within, without—
And ever turn my face about
To see if Death is stalking me;

Death, who will lead me, when he please,
Where one called Pluto takes his ease,
Welcoming to his dismal den
Any and all who venture thence;
Easy to enter, ah! but whence
Never does one return again.

Le Quatriesme Livre des Odes, XIII

Ode

Pourquoy chetif laboureur
Trembles-tu d'un Empereur,
Qui doit bien tost, legere ombre,
Des morts accroistre le nombre?
"Ne sçais-tu qu'à tout chacun★
Le port d'Enfer est commun,
Et qu'une ame Imperiale
Aussi tost là bas devale
Dans le bateau de Charon,†
Que l'ame d'un bucheron?"

Courage coupeur de terre!
Ces grans foudres de la guerre
Non plus que toy n'iront pas
Armez d'un plastron là bas,
Comme ils alloyent aux batailles:
Autant leur vaudront leurs mailles,
Leurs lances et leur estoc,
Comme à toy vaudra ton soc

Le bon juge Rhadamante‡
Asseuré ne s'espouvante
Non plus de voir un harnois
Là bas, qu'un levier de bois,
Ou voir une souquenie
Qu'une robbe bien garnie,
Ou qu'un riche accoustrement
D'un Roy mort pompeusement.

★It is not clear exactly why Ronsard sets off these lines in quotation marks, but I follow him in doing so. [NRS]

†See p. 311.

‡Rhadamanthus, son of Zeus and Europa, was, with his brothers Minos and Aeacus, one of the judges of the underworld, rewarded for the justice he meted out on earth. [NRS]

Ode

Lowly ploughman, friend, wherefore
Fear you so an Emperor,
One who, soon, an airy ghost,
Will join death's increasing host?
"For, when all is said and done,
Know you not that everyone—
Soul of woodsman, soul of king—
Must pass through the opening
To the netherworld, with him
Whose bark plies the river grim?"

Take heart, you who plough the land!
Those great warriors, doughty band,
Heroes stout, I guarantee,
Will not clothed in armor be,
Anymore than you; nor, now,
Need your ploughshare and your plough,
Howsoever commonplace,
Bow to mail, and spear, and mace.

Rhadamanthus' judgment will
Not be swayed by martial frill
Or equipment military
Anymore than ordinary
Wooden plough-shaft of your trade;
Nor will he be much dismayed
By the sight of ragged clothes
Rather than rich furbelows,
Or the robes and filigrees
Of King's sumptuous obsequies.

Le Quatriesme Livre des Odes, XIV

Ode

Lors que Bacchus entre chez moy
Je chasse incontinent l'esmoy,
Et ravi d'esprit il me semble
Qu'en mes bougettes j'ay plus d'or,
Plus d'argent, et plus de tresor
Que Mide, ny que Crœse ensemble.

Je ne veux rien sinon tourner
Par la danse, et me couronner
Le chef d'un tortis de lierre:
Je foule en esprit les honneurs,
Et les estats des grands Seigneurs
À coups de pied j'escraze à terre.

Page, verse du vin nouveau,
Arrache-moy hors du cerveau
Le soin, par qui le cœur me tombe.
Verse donc pour me l'arracher:
Il vaut mieux yvre se coucher
Dans le lict, que mort dans la tombe.

Ode

When Bacchus comes to visit me,
Gone in a trice is my ennui.
My spirit soars, I doubt not whether
Filled are my pockets with more gold,
More silver, and more wealth untold
Than Midas' and Croesus', altogether.

Naught would I do but dance, my head
Crowned round, with ivy garlanded;
And in my mind I scorn, confound
All worldly honors, now inclined
To stamp my feet, the while, and grind
Our Lordships' states into the ground.

Page, pour a glass of fine young wine;
Purge from my brain all dark design,
All care that would my heart consume.
Pour it, and be they purged; for I
Sooner a drunken sot would lie,
In bed, than dead and in the tomb.

Le Quatriesme Livre des Odes, XXIV

Ode anacréontique*

La terre les eaux va boivant,
L'arbre la boit par sa racine,
La mer salée boit le vent,
Et le Soleil boit la marine,

Le Soleil est beu de la Lune:
Tout boit, soit en haut ou en bas:
Suivant ceste reigle commune
Pourquoy donc ne boirons-nous pas?

*The influence of Greek poet Anacreon, whose dates (ca. 582–ca. 485 B.C.E.) are a matter of some dispute, from the Middle Ages and long after far outweighed the rather few fragments of his actual production to have survived. Though he was thought to have written a collection of odes celebrating the joys of wine, women, and song, that attribution is now known to be false. (A telling example of his far-ranging influence can be seen in the fact that the tune of "The Star-Spangled Banner" was originally an old English drinking song entitled "To Anacreon in Heaven.") [NRS]

Anacreontic Ode

The earth drinks rain, and drinks its fill,
The thirsting root drinks for the tree,
The sea drinks in the wind until
The Sun, in turn, drinks up the sea,

The Moon drinks in the Sun's fair light;
Everything drinks, both low and high:
If this be true, is it not right
That we drink too, both you and I?

Le Quatriesme Livre des Odes, XXXI

Ode

Je suis homme nay pour mourir,
Je suis bien seur que du trespas
Je ne me sçaurois secourir
Que poudre je n'aille là bas.

Je cognois bien les ans que j'ay:
Mais ceux qui me doivent venir
Bons ou mauvais, je ne les sçay,
Ny quand mon âge doit finir.

Pour-ce fuyez-vous-en esmoy,
Qui rongez mon cœur à tous coups,
Fuyez-vous-en bien loin de moy,
Je n'ay que faire avecque vous.

Aumoins avant que trespasser,
Que je puisse à mon aise un jour
Jouer, sauter, rire et danser
Avecque Bacchus et Amour.

Ode

Mortal am I, man born to die;
Certain am I, in time, death must
Prevail, just as, most surely, I,
Do what I may, will turn to dust.

I know the years that I have had:
But those that I have yet to spend,
I know not, whether good or bad,
Nor when my age will reach its end.

Wherefore I tell you, wrack and woe,
Who gnaw my heart: "Be off! Adieu!
Be off, as far as you can go,
For naught have I to do with you."

At least, before I die, I pray
One day, whatever may betide,
That I may laugh, and dance, and play,
With Love and Bacchus by my side.

Le Quatriesme Livre des Odes, XXXIX

Ode

Ma Maistresse, que j'aime mieux
Dix mille fois ny que mes yeux,
Ny que mon cœur, ny que ma vie,
Ne me donne plus, je te prie,
Des confitures pour manger,
Pensant ma fiévre soulager.
Car ta confiture, Mignonne,
Tant elle est douce, ne me donne
Qu'un desir de tousjours vouloir
Estre malade, pour avoir
Tes friandises en la bouche.
Mais bien si quelque ennuy te touche
De me voir ainsi tourmenté
Pour la perte de ma santé,
Et si tu veux que dés ceste heure,
Pour vivre dedans toy, je meure,
Fay moy serment par Cupidon,
Par ses traits et par son brandon,
Et par son arc et par sa trousse,
Et par Venus qui est si douce
À celles qui gardent leur foy,
Que jamais un autre que moy,

Ode

My Mistress, whom I idolize
Ten thousand times more than my eyes,
Or than my heart, or than my very
Life, I beseech you, no more berry
Jellies and jams, no matter how
You think they cool my fevered brow!
For your preserves are sweet, my Pet;
So sweet that I would gladly let
Myself be ever ailing, thus
To eat and eat them, gluttonous.
But if you are distressed, distraught,
Shuddering merely at the thought
That I am ill, most painfully,
And if you wish that I might be
Healthy enough of flesh and sinew
To hug, gasp, sigh, and die within you,
Then swear by Cupid—by his brand,
His bow, his darts, his quiver—and
By Venus, who treats gently those
Belles ever faithful to their beaus:
Swear that no other, even some
Adonis fair, will ever come

Fust-ce un Adonis, n'aura place
Et ton heureuse bonne grace:
Lors ton serment pourra guarir
La fiévre qui me fait mourir,
Et non ta douce confiture,
Qui ne m'est que vaine pasture.

Before myself in your affection.
For such an oath will my dejection
Cure, and my deathly fever ease,
More swiftly, surely, than all these
Preserves: confections that you send me,
Which please my taste but will not mend me.

Le Cinquiesme Livre des Odes, XXVI

Odelette

Ce-pendant que ce beau mois dure,
Mignonne, allon sur la verdure,
Ne laisson perdre en vain le temps:
L'âge glissant qui ne s'arreste,
Meslant le poil de nostre teste,
S'enfuit ainsi que le Printemps.

Donq ce pendant que nostre vie
Et le Temps d'aimer nous convie
Aimon, moissonnon nos desirs,
Passon l'Amour de veine en veine:
Incontinent la mort prochaine
Viendra derober nos plaisirs.

Odelet

Whilst fair the season, let us not,
Let time fly useless, misbegot,
My pet: come to the greenery;
For age, in endless flow, slips by,
Turning me gray before your eye,
Passing like Springtime, fleetingly.

Wherefore, whilst life and Time invite,
Offering Love for our delight,
Come gather we our hearts' desires;
Let them go coursing through our veins:
For too soon naught but death remains,
To steal the pleasures, quell the fires.

Le Cinquiesme Livre des Odes, XXVIII

Ode

Tay toy babillarde Arondelle,
Ou bien je plumeray ton aile
Si je t'empongne, ou d'un couteau
Je te couperay la languette,
Qui matin sans repos caquette,
Et m'estourdit tout le cerveau.

Je te preste ma cheminée
Pour chanter toute la journée,
De soir de nuict quand tu voudras:
Mais au matin ne me reveille,
Et ne m'oste quand je sommeille
Ma Cassandre d'entre mes bras.

Ode

Hush, Swallow! Stop your jabbering,
Lest I pluck bare your feathered wing,
If I can catch you, or cut out
Your little tongue, which, morning long,
Cackles its neverending song
And jars my weary brain about.

I have no quarrel when you use
My chimney any time you choose,
By day or night, as suits you best:
But in the morning let me sleep;
And, sleeping, let me dream I keep
Cassandra clasped tight to my breast.

Le Cinquiesme Livre des Odes, XXX★

★This poem, not to be confused with another bearing the same number in Book 5 of *Les Odes* ("En vous donnant ce portrait mien"), was apparently included in the 1560 edition of the *Œuvres* and subsequently removed from that of 1567. Céard-Ménager-Simonin includes it under the rubric "Pièces de 1560 retranchées en 1567." [NRS]

LES MASCARADES, COMBATS
ET CARTELS

Pour le Roy François*

SECOND DE CE NOM, ALORS NOMMÉ ROY-DAUPHIN

On ne voit point qu'un fort Lion ne face
Ses lionneaux hardis et furieux:
Ce jeune Roy sorty de bonne race
Aura le cœur pareil à ses ayeux.

*As the title indicates, the subject of this adulation is François II (1544–1560), son of Henri II and Catherine de Médicis, and husband of Mary, Queen of Scots. The quatrain, as well as the following one, in fulsome praise of the latter, is one of two dozen such bits of occasional verse withdrawn from the 1584 edition of the *Œuvres*. (See Céard-Ménager-Simonin 2: 1388–1389.) [NRS]

For King François
SECOND OF THAT NAME, LATER NAMED ROI-DAUPHIN

Rare would it be a Lion strong to see,
Whose cubs, too meek, could neither rage nor roar:
This young King, noble race's progeny,
Will have the heart of those who came before.

Les Mascarades, combats et cartels

Pour la Royne d'Escosse,

ALORS ROYNE DE FRANCE

Ainsi qu'on voit demy-blanche et vermeille
Naistre l'Aurore, et Vesper sur la nuit,
Ainsi sur toute en beauté nompareille
Des Escossois la Princesse reluit.

For the Queen of Scotland

LATER QUEEN OF FRANCE

Like tender whites and reds we see when Morn
Dawns in the sky and Dusk announces night,
Just so, when she of matchless beauty born,
The Princess of the Scots, sheds forth her light.

Les Mascarades, combats et cartels

LE BOCAGE

Vœu d'un chemineur à une fontaine★

Pour m'estre dedans ton onde,
Fonteine, desalteré
Or' que le chien aitheré
De soif tourmente le monde,
J'éleve à tes bors champestres
En trofée, pour guerdon,
Et ma gourde, et mon bourdon,
Ma panetiere, et mes guestres.

★See pp. 234ff.

A Traveler's Vow to a Fountain

Fountain, in these dog days' heat
That besets the world accursed,
Since you let me slake my thirst,
It is only right and meet
That I hang, by your green banks,
These, my leggings, pipes, and gourd,
And my sack of bread: reward
That I give you with my thanks.

Le Bocage★

★The thirteen poems originally published under the title *Le Bocage* in
1550 and 1554, and subsequently withdrawn from the Œuvres, are included
in Céard-Ménager-Simonin under the rubric "Pièces mêlées antérieures à
1560 et non recueillies dans *Les Œuvres.*" [NRS]

D'un pasteur au dieu Pan

De ma brebis ecorchée,
Morte entre les dens du lou,
À toi j'apen à ce clou
La dépouille pour trofée.
Ô Dieu Pan, si quelque grace
T'emeut en lieu de ceci,
Donne m'en cet an icy
Un cent d'autres en sa place.

From a Shepherd to the God Pan

As a tribute, Pan, to you,
My ewe's carcass here I hang,
She who fell to wolf's sharp fang,
Whom the beast held fast and slew.
Worthy god! If this scapegrace
Moves your heart to tenderness,
Pray give me this year no less
Than a hundred in her place.

Le Bocage

D'une courtizanne à Venus

Si je puis ma jeunesse folle,
Hantant les bordeaus, garentir
De ne pouvoir jamais sentir
Ne poulains, chancre, ne verole,

Ô Venus, de Bacus compaigne,
À toi je promets en mes vœus
Mon éponge, et mes faus cheveus,
Mon fard, mon miroer, et mon paigne.

From a Courtesan to Venus

If, by whatever artifice,
You guard my youth, in brothel spent—
My foolish youth, on pleasure bent—
From sore, and scab, and syphilis,

I promise to bequeath to you,
Consort of Bacchus, Venus fair,
My puff, my artificial hair,
My rouge, my comb, my mirror too.

Le Bocage

LES POEMES

Epigramme, à Julien★

Toujours tu me prêches, Julien,
Que je ne parle que de boire,
Et que ce n'est pas le moyen
De m'aquerir ny biens, ny gloire:

Mais répons, gentil glorieux,
(Je veux defendre mon afaire)
Répons moy, ne vaut-il pas mieux
En écrire, que de le faire?

★This poem, originally part of an early collection, was included in the 1560 edition of the *Œuvres* but was subsequently deleted. It appears in Céard-Ménager-Simonin under the rubric "Pièces de la section des 'Poèmes' des 'Œuvres' (1560), retranchées en 1567," the notes to which theorize (2:1545) that the Julien addressed may have been one Julien Peccate, an ecclesiastic from Le Mans, whose name crops up from time to time in Ronsard's chronology. The same notes suggest that his supposed reply (following) was, in all likelihood, composed by Ronsard himself. [NRS]

Epigram, to Julien

You preach that all I speak about,
Julien, is drinking, and decree
That never, in no wise, no doubt,
Will that enrich or honor me:

But tell me (you who thus indict),
Honored friend, if I misconstrue:
Is it not better, far, to write
About it than to do it too?

Les Poemes

Responce de Julien

Tu veux avecques ton bel art
Du bon sophiste contrefaire:
Il ne faudroit, gentil Ronsard,
Ny en écrire, ny le faire.

Julien's Reply

Despite your art, Ronsard, dear friend,
Your sophistry has little to it:
For neither ought we, in the end,
To write about it or to do it.

Les Poemes

Imitation de Martial*

Ha mauditte nature! hé, pourquoy m'as tu fait
Si dextrement formé d'esprit et de corsage?
Que ne m'as tu fait nain, ou chevelu sauvage?
Niez, badin, ou fol, ou monstre contrefait?

Si j'estois nain j'aurois toute chose à souhait,
J'aurois soixante sols par jour et d'avantage,
J'aurois faveur du Roy, caresse, et bon visage,
Bien en point, bien vestu, bien gras, et bien refait.

Ah! que vous fustes fols, mes parents, de me faire
Pauvre escolier Latin! vous deviez contrefaire
Mon corps, ou me nourrir à l'escole des fous.

Ah! ingrates chansons! ah! malheureuses Muses!
Rompez moy par depit fleuttes et cornemuses,
Puis qu'aujourd'huy les nains sont plus heureus que nous.

---

*This sonnet, like the "Epigramme, à Julien," had appeared earlier in another collection before being assigned definitively, though not permanently, since, like others of its group, it was eventually withdrawn. The informative note in Céard-Ménager-Simonin (2:1545) does not, however, explain the specific reference to Martial. [NRS]

Imitation of Martial

Ah, cursèd nature! Why did you decide
To fashion me so hale of mind and breast?
Why not a dwarf? Why not some beast unblest,
Shaggy, wild, daft; some monster ogrified?*

Were I a dwarf, naught would I be denied:
I would have sixty sous a day, caressed
By King and court; be plump, well dressed,
Bedecked, beprized,* and much beloved beside.

Ah, foolish parents, who my youth misspent
With Latin! Best had they misshapen, bent
My limbs, or schooled me in stupidity!

Ah, useless songs! Ah, Muses, worthless brutes!
Dashed to bits be my damnèd pipes, my flutes,
Since dwarfs, today, are happier, far, than we!

Les Poemes

*Readers who may take issue with the words *ogrified* and *beprized* are reminded that one of the important contributions of Ronsard and the other poets of the Pléiade was their willingness to coin neologisms. [NRS]

TRADUCTION DE QUELQUES
EPIGRAMMES GRECZ

De Palladas★

Ô mere des flateurs, Richesse,
Fille de soin et de tristesse,
T'avoir est une grande peur
Et ne t'avoir grande douleur.

★Two of five brief pieces translated by Ronsard from the *Greek Anthology*
and included in the Céard-Ménager-Simonin edition under the rubric
"Pièces de la section des 'Poèmes' des 'Œuvres' (1573), retranchées en 1578,"
are from the pen of Palladas, the fifth-century Epicurean who, with some
150 epigrams, including the present one (IX, cccxcv), was the single most
prolific poet represented in that work. (See Jacobs, *Anthologie grecque,* 2:394–
395.) [NRS]

O Wealth, who flatterers beget,
Daughter of care and sad regret,
Great fear has he who has you got,
And great distress, who has you not.

Traduction de quelques epigrammes grecz

De Lucil★

Ayant tel crochet de naseaux
Fuy les fonteines et les eaux,
Et ne te mires en leur bord:
Si ton visage tu mirois,
Comme Narcisse tu mourrois,
Te haïssant jusqu'à la mort.

★The Lucil referred to, not to be confused with Caius Lucilius, the father
of Latin satire, was apparently one Loukillios, a Greek of Roman ancestry at
the time of Nero, author of twenty-four epigrams in the *Greek Anthology,*
including the original of Ronsard's present quatrain (XI, LXXVI). (See Jacobs,
Anthologie grecque, 2:375–376.) [NRS]

With those two nostrils in that hook,
Flee fountain, lake, and flowing brook;
Gaze not, Narcissus-like, therein:
For if, upon too close inspection,
You were to spy your fell reflection,
Self-hate, not love, would do you in.

Traduction de quelques epigrammes grecz

Epitaphe de Nicolas Vergece, grec★

Crete me fist, la France m'a nourry,
La Normandie ici me tient pourry.
Ô fier Destin qui les hommes tourmente,
Qui fais un Grec à Coutance perir!
"Ainsi prend fin toute chose naissante:†
De quelque part qu'on puisse ici mourir,
Un seul chemin nous meine à Rhadamante."‡

★Vergèce, a friend of Ronsard's, was a minor poet and humanist of the period, dead in 1570 in the Normandie town of Coutances. [NRS]

†On Ronsard's seemingly capricious use of quotation marks, compare p. 338, note. [NRS]

‡See p. 338, note.

Epitaph for Nicolas Vergèce, a Greek

Crete gave me birth, France suckled, nourished me,
And here I lie, rotting, in Normandie.
O Fate, who clutch man in your haughty thrall,
Who make a Greek come to Coutances to die!
"Thus every living thing, in time, must fall:
Wherever, on this earth, our bones may lie,
One road to Rhadamanthus leads us all."

Epitaphes de divers sujets

Epitaphe de Thomas★

La volupté, la gourmandise,
Le vin et le discord aussi,
Et l'une et l'autre paillardise
Avec Thomas gisent icy.

En lieu d'une moisson partie
D'entre les fleurs du renouveau,
Tousjours le chardon et l'ortie
Puisse esgrafigner son tombeau.

★The identity of the profligate Thomas has, to my knowledge, never been unearthed. [NRS]

Epitaph for Thomas

Here lechery and gluttony,
Discord and drink—and, little wonder,
Many another infamy—
Lie buried with Thomas, hereunder.

Instead of flowers in springtime picked
And spread about, behind, before,
Let be his grave by brambles pricked,
Thistles, and thorns, forevermore.

Epitaphes de divers sujets

Epitaphe de Jaques Mernable, joueur de farces*

Tandis que tu vivois, Mernable,
Tu n'avois ny maison ny table,
Et jamais, pauvre, tu n'as veu
En ta maison le pot au feu.

Ores la mort t'est profitable:
Car tu n'as plus besoin de table
Ny de pot, et si desormais
Tu as maison pour tout jamais.

*No details appear to be known concerning the subject of this epitaph, which had a variety of printings throughout Ronsard's lifetime. (See Céard-Ménager-Simonin 2:1567–1568.) [NRS]

Epitaph of Jaques Mernable, Player of Tricks

Mernable, when alive you were,
Table nor house were yours, monsieur;
And since a *pauvre diable* were you,
You never saw a pot of stew.

Today does death its goods confer:
No table need you now, monsieur,
Nor pot; as for a house, however,
Now have you one that lasts forever.

Epitaphes de divers sujets

ILLUSTRATION CREDITS

Page 20: Jean Jacques Boissard, *Bibliotheca chalcographica, illustrium virtute atque eruditione in tota Europa, clarissimorum virorum* (Frankfurt: Johannis Ammonii Bibliopola, 1650–1654). Courtesy of the Burndy Library, Dibner Institute for the History of Science and Technology, Cambridge, Massachusetts

Page 75: Konrad Gesner, *Thierbuch; das ist, ein kurtze bschreybung aller vierfuessigen thieren* . . . (Zurich: Froschower, 1563). Courtesy of the Burndy Library, Dibner Institute for the History of Science and Technology, Cambridge, Massachusetts

Page 108: *Le Tombeav de Margverite de Valois royne de Navarre: Faict premierement en disticques latins,* edited by Nicolas Denisot (Paris: De l'imprimerie de Michel Fezandat, & Robert Granion, 1551). By permission of the Houghton Library, Harvard University

Page 158: Joachim du Bellay, *Les Oevvres françoises de Ioachim Dv Bellay* (Paris: Par Federic Morel, 1584). By permission of the Houghton Library, Harvard University

Page 187: Sebastiano Serlio, *Des Antiquites, Le troisiesme liure translate d'italien en franchois* (Antwerp: Pierre Coeck d'Alost, par Gil. van Diest, 1550). By permission of the Houghton Library, Harvard University

Page 213: Jean Dorat, *Magnificentissimj spectaculi, a regina regum matre in hortis suburbanis editi, in Henrici regis Poloniae inuictissimi nuper renunciati gratulationem, descriptio* (Paris: Ex O cina F ederici Morelli, 1573). By permission of the Houghton Library, Harvard University

Page 245: Konrad Gesner, *Thierbuch; das ist, ein kurtze bschreybung aller vierfuessigen thieren* . . . (Zurich: Froschower, 1563). Courtesy of the Burndy Library, Dibner Institute for the History of Science and Technology, Cambridge, Massachusetts

Page 266: Pierre de Ronsard, *Les Oevvres de Pierre de Ronsard gentilhomme vandomois, prince des poètes françois. Reueues et augmentées* (Paris: Chez Nicolas Bvon, 1609). By permission of the Houghton Library, Harvard University

Page 329: Pierre de Ronsard, *Les figvres et povrtraictz des sept a'ages de l'homme* (Paris, 1580), pl. 3, "Adolesence," engraved after original by Baptiste Pellerin. By permission of the Houghton Library, Harvard University

Page 371: Jean Dorat, *Magnificentissimj spectaculi, a regina regum matre in hortis suburbanis editi, in Henrici regis Poloniae inuictissimi nuper renunciati gratulationem, descriptio* (Paris: Ex O cina F ederici Morelli, 1573). By permission of the Houghton Library, Harvard University

NORMAN R. SHAPIRO is professor of Romance languages and literatures at Wesleyan University. Among his many translations are *Four Farces* by Georges Feydeau, which was nominated for a National Book Award, *The Fabulists French: Verse Fables of Nine Centuries,* named Distinguished Book of the Year by the American Literary Translators' Association, *Fifty Fables of La Fontaine, One Hundred and One Poems by Paul Verlaine,* and Charles Baudelaire: *Selected Poems from "Les Fleurs du mal,"* the last two published by the University of Chicago Press.

HOPE GLIDDEN teaches French at Tulane University where she is the Kathryn B. Gore professor of French. She has published widely on Renaissance writing, including Rabelais, Marguerite de Navarre, and Montaigne, on French historiography, and is currently writing a book on the notion of *patrimoine* in the information age.